Breaking into Factual TV

Successfully entering the TV industry can be difficult to navigate. *Breaking into Factual TV* will guide you through the process from how to get your first job to how to make it at the top.

Writing in a clear and accessible way, author Zenia Selby demystifies the TV industry for new entrants and covers all the key roles, including runner, researcher, assistant producer, producer and director. Selby reveals what no one ever tells you when you start working at a TV production company – the chain of hierarchy, the most effective ways to network and the best way to structure your work. The book will travel with you up your career ladder: as you progress from runner to researcher to producer to director, each section provides you with the blueprint you need to excel with every promotion and warns you of the pitfalls to avoid. Perspectives from industry professionals are provided throughout, with interviews with Mitch Langcaster-James (*The Only Way is Essex*, *QI* and *Celebs Go Dating*), Jeremy Turner (*Edward Snowden: Whistleblower or Spy?* and *Women in Prison*), Alec Lindsell (*Inside the Factory* and *The One Show*) and Sophie Smith (*Albert: The Power Behind Victoria* and *Digging for Britain*) to offer insight into the reality of their roles.

The book is ideal for emerging professionals and graduates of television courses looking to take their first step in the TV industry.

Zenia Selby is an award-winning Creative Producer who specialises in history documentaries. She has produced films for a variety of international broadcasters, including the BBC, Discovery Channel, Netflix and Al Jazeera.

Breaking into Factual TV

Your Career Companion

Zenia Selby

Routledge
Taylor & Francis Group

LONDON AND NEW YORK

Designed cover image: Illustrations by Cressida Peever at CressidaCards

First published 2023
by Routledge
4 Park Square, Milton Park, Abingdon, Oxon OX14 4RN

and by Routledge
605 Third Avenue, New York, NY 10158

Routledge is an imprint of the Taylor & Francis Group, an informa business

British Library Cataloguing-in-Publication Data
A catalogue record for this book is available from the British Library

Library of Congress Cataloging-in-Publication Data
Names: Selby, Zenia, author.
Title: Breaking into factual TV : your career companion / Zenia Selby.
Description: Abingdon, Oxon ; New York, NY : Routledge, 2023. | Includes index.
Identifiers: LCCN 2022054824 (print) | LCCN 2022054825 (ebook) |
ISBN 9781032277714 (hardback) | ISBN 9781032277691 (paperback) |
ISBN 9781003294009 (ebook)
Subjects: LCSH: Television–Production and direction–Vocational guidance.
Classification: LCC PN1992.75 .S45 2023 (print) | LCC PN1992.75 (ebook) |
DDC 791.4502/3207–dc23/eng/20221213
LC record available at https://lccn.loc.gov/2022054824
LC ebook record available at https://lccn.loc.gov/2022054825

ISBN: 9781032277714 (hbk)
ISBN: 9781032277691 (pbk)
ISBN: 9781003294009 (ebk)

DOI: 10.4324/9781003294009

Typeset in Sabon
by Newgen Publishing UK

Contents

Introduction

Why you need this book

Some industries have a clear application process and obvious career path. Take law, for example. You do a law degree, you apply to law firms, you become a lawyer. With the television industry, on the other hand, it's much harder to know where to start. That's where this book comes in.

How to use this book

This book is designed to give you step-by-step support as you make your way through a career in Factual TV. I would recommend reading Chapters 1–3 before you start applying for jobs, then keeping this book with you as you work your way through the industry. Always read one chapter ahead of where you are in your career – that way you can work on developing the skills you need for your next step up.

Remember that this is not an exhaustive list of all the different jobs you could be doing in the TV industry. You may find, as you gain experience, that you want to specialise in a specific aspect of TV production – archive, or question writing or fact checking. Equally, you may find that you want to step sideways from editorial to production, or perhaps you prefer making branded content to broadcast. Perhaps you'll use the skills you develop in the TV industry to specialise in social media production or short films. Whatever you decide to do, this book will guarantee you a strong grounding in the skills you need to make yourself transferable, valuable and professional.

Throughout this book, we'll hear from several TV professionals about their own career paths and experiences. Everyone's journey is slightly different, as you'll see – so don't worry about following a career path that's 'by the book'. However, what's common to each contributor is that they use their skills and backgrounds to their advantage, transferring them to their TV jobs, and they make sure they learn something new from each project

DOI: 10.4324/9781003294009-1

they work on. This is an important mindset that will set you up to be a better professional.

Below is a guideline for the minimum number of years you should aim to spend in each role on the editorial ladder. Less than this and you may not have gained sufficient experience to prepare you for the next step. You are always welcome to spend more years in each role, but unless you make a conscious decision to stay in that position because you enjoy it, you run the risk of getting stuck at that level.

Runner – 1 year
Researcher – 2 years
Assistant Producer – 3 years
Producer – unlimited
Director – unlimited

Now go ahead – turn the page and find out where to start!

Chapter 1

Breaking in

The television industry is a network-based industry. This means that you're much more likely to get a job through personal connections than you are through an official application process. This kind of system causes obvious issues: elitism, nepotism and financial barriers to entry. On the other hand, people skills are important in this industry: if you have the skills to network your way into a job, it's likely that you will flourish in television.

In this chapter, I will guide you through the ways in which you can start to build that network. I'll also warn you of some of the less ethical practices in television, such as unpaid internships, and advise you of ways in which you can still get a foot in the door without having to compromise your financial situation. Finally, I'll help you lay out your CV in a TV-friendly way, pick which genre to work in and decide where to live to maximise your TV career.

Networking

The first place to start networking is with any personal contacts you have. Do you know anyone who works in TV? Do your parents or friends know anyone? They may not work in the genre you're interested in, or they may do a job that's linked to TV but not in TV production – it doesn't matter, just politely ask them to meet for coffee and express your interest in the industry. They may just be the first link in the chain that leads to a job.

Next on the to-do list is to email production companies that produce the kind of television you're interested in making. It is best to try and identify a real person working at the company and email them, rather than generic office@ or info@ email addresses – those will go to the office manager or office runner, who will most likely ignore it, unless the company has a specific policy of accepting and considering unsolicited CVs. See if you can find a talent manager or head of production at the companies and email them directly. If you can't find anyone through searching on the internet, phone up the production company and ask to whom you should send your CV. Make sure you put your name and the kind of job you want (e.g. runner,

DOI: 10.4324/9781003294009-2

researcher) in the subject line – that will immediately grab the recipient's attention if they happen to be crewing up and need someone like you. Do not email them with an essay in the body of the email – a couple of sentences will suffice, something along the lines of:

> Dear X, my name is Y, I am [a recent graduate] looking for work as a runner/researcher [delete as appropriate]. I previously worked on [cite relevant experience] and am available from [date]. I have attached my CV for your reference.

The networking method that has worked best for me has been to attend events such as film screenings, film festivals, networking nights or drinks parties. Signing up to TV-related newsletters, such as those published by Women in Film and TV, RTS or BAFTA, will keep you well informed of such opportunities. Twitter is also a good place to find out about events. Talk to as many people as you can while you are there and get their contact details to add to your spreadsheet. Follow up with any you feel might be able to help you get a job. The least awkward or self-serving way to do this is to research their background, come up with a question that you know they are well equipped to answer (such as 'how do you balance filming documentary and drama?', 'I'm interested in becoming a researcher, can you tell me what that's like' or 'I'm thinking of shooting a short in Venezuela – I see your latest project involved filming in that country; can you give me any tips on how to set up a shoot there?'), then email the question and offer to buy them a coffee. This is just the icebreaker though – the most rewarding connections happen when there is no clear agenda on either side, just the opportunity to develop a professional friendship, share opinions and interests, and have a fun and stimulating conversation. Try to avoid reciting your CV and certainly do not ask your contact to recite theirs (you should already be familiar with their experience). However, if it should come up, do try to drop any relevant experience into your conversation, as this will help them to compartmentalise you and keep you in mind for similar job opportunities.

Internships

If you are currently in full-time education and financially supported, then by all means go ahead and sign up for as many work experience placements as you possibly can. You can even email production companies that don't have overt work experience schemes or programmes and offer yourself up for a placement.

However, if you are not in full-time education, you should not be doing unpaid work. The TV industry is notorious for taking advantage of unpaid interns, which of course creates a financial barrier to entry – only those who can support themselves can take up these internships – which in turn contributes to TV's diversity problem. Know your rights: if you are offered an internship, you are entitled to ask to be paid the minimum wage during your placement. Some production companies will offer expenses instead (train tickets and lunches). It is up to you whether you decide to take this or ask for the minimum wage. If you are offered a job following your work experience placement, you should ask to be back paid for the duration of your placement.

There are several organisations working to combat TV's addiction to unpaid work experience placements, as well as programmes that support new entrants without compromising their financial security. A few of these are listed below:

Internship schemes and training programmes

- **BBC**
  The BBC offers the Production Trainee Scheme and the Production Apprenticeship. The Apprenticeship is open to those without a degree; the Trainee Scheme is open to those with or without a degree. The scheme is highly competitive but offers successful applicants a complete overview of the different genres of TV produced by the BBC. If you're clear on exactly which genre you want to work in, this may not be for you, but if you're not sure and want to try a few out within the prestigious and well-connected environment of the BBC, then make sure you set an alert for their application deadlines.

- **Grierson DocLab**
  This is an incredible programme for 18–25-year-olds that covers every genre of Factual TV and provides unparalleled training, workshops and paid placements at production companies. This should be top of your application list.

- **The Network**
  This programme gives sixty places annually to people who are passionate about working in TV and are completely new to the industry. The Network offers workshops, networking sessions and mentoring, which all take place across four days in August at the Edinburgh TV Festival (which follows the Edinburgh Fringe). Everything, including accommodation and food, is covered by The Network.

- **ITV**
  ITV offers a New Traineeship and a Technology Graduate Scheme, as well as work experience placements and runner opportunities.

- **RDF**

  RDF Television offers five interns each year a paid internship that feeds them directly into productions at the company.

- **Sky**

  Sky offers a wide range of opportunities and is a great place to get started. Bear in mind that their offices are on the outskirts of London – which is great if you're moving to the city for the internship, as the outskirts are more affordable, but won't give you the buzz of central London.

Remember that you are not always guaranteed a job straight after you finish the internship. You will need to use these programmes to build your network and learn as much as possible about the industry. Make sure you keep a spreadsheet of the contact details of people you meet. Ask them for a follow-up coffee or update them with your CV regularly. By regularly, I mean either every three to six months, or whenever you gain a new credit.

Writing your CV

The primary aim of your CV is to allow employers to **identify, verify** and **contact** you. Employers in TV spend between 10 and 30 seconds looking at CVs. This means it needs to command their attention and convey relevant information quickly. Here are a few dos and don'ts about how to lay out your CV in a TV-friendly format:

DO put your name at the top. In big letters, so people can easily see whose CV they're reading.

DON'T include your picture. It's not your social media profile, and anyway this helps to prevent unconscious bias.

DO put your industry level – and make it appropriate for the job you're applying for. So don't put 'Sam Jones – Producer' if you're applying for a researcher job, even if you have already produced some short films!

DO put a little mission statement – but only if it's a good one. A bad mission statement is worse than no mission statement at all. This should just be a couple of sentences that's like a trailer for your CV, highlighting your best credits and top skills. Maybe try asking a friend to write it for you – they may highlight things about you that you have missed! You can then use this mission statement across other professional platforms, like LinkedIn and the Talent Manager.

DO put your contact details – email address and phone number are fine, plus a website if you have one.

DON'T put your address. Firstly, you shouldn't be disclosing such personal details; secondly, it might genuinely cost you a job – for example, you're applying for something in south-west London but live in north London. That's an 80-minute commute, and a kindly production manager may well try to save you the trouble by rejecting your application.

DO put your skills in a list or table right at the top of your CV. This can include things like self-shooting, editing software with which you're familiar, a clean driving licence, training courses you've been on, etc.

DO head up each credit with a straightforward top line: Company name, Production name, Role, Dates of employment.

DO mention the director, series producer or exec you worked with on each production, or include them as references after your top line. Your potential employer will call them up if they know them and ask what you were like to work with. So logically –

DON'T put down anyone on your CV with whom you didn't have a good professional relationship. If your potential employer knows them, they'll ring them – and that person may not give you the best recommendation.

DON'T put your references at the end of your CV. Your potential employer probably won't read all the way to the end.

DON'T include every exam you've ever taken as your qualifications. No one cares whether or not you did Spanish GCSE – unless it's relevant to the job you're applying for, in which case put it in your cover letter or email. Keep your qualifications to your latest ones, e.g. A levels, BTEC, IB or university/college degree.

DO save a copy as a pdf, to prevent any change in the formatting on different operating systems.

DON'T make your CV longer than two pages. If you run out of space for your credits, then add a little note, such as: 'Please contact me for full details of all runner credits from [date you ran out of space] to [date you had your first job].'

Here is an extract from my CV, as an example. I, in turn, based this on a sample CV that was sent to me by a talent manager at the BBC, which she liked to use as an example of the best laid out CV she had ever received. You can adapt this to suit you – for example, removing the mission statement, perhaps using a table format for your credits or including a list of cameras you can shoot on. However, I've noticed that many of my colleagues use this basic layout, as it conveys a lot of information quickly. Choose a formatting style that reflects a bit of your personality, but still looks professional.

Zenia Selby

Producer

I am a Producer with extensive experience across specialist factual productions and development. Having worked for both broadcast commissioners and corporate clients, I am capable of framing stories for a variety of audiences, and structuring both long- form and short-form content. I have produced shoots on the ground both in the UK and abroad, working with high-profile talent in challenging environments. Recently, a short documentary I produced and directed, titled *Painting Freedom*, won Best International Documentary at the 300 Seconds Film Festival.

Contact   zenia.selby@gmail.com   https://vimeo.com/zeniaselby

Experience

SHELL CONTENT ENGINE, *Producer*, May 5th – December 16th 2021
Reference: [excised]
I worked on a number of different projects with Shell, collaborating with stakeholders across the company to produce short-form films both for internal and external audiences that fit with the company's overall communications strategy.

WORLD MEDIA RIGHTS, *Producer Director*, **Royals in Colour (Curiosity Stream)**, March 1st – April 16th 2021
Reference: [excised]
I worked on Episode 6, writing the scripts, directing the interviews and edit producing to rough cut.

WAG ENTERTAINMENT, *Location Producer*, **What on Earth S7 (Science Channel)**, September 28th 2020 – February 26th 2021
Reference: [excised]

I set up the location shoots for all twenty stories in this series, which were filmed all over the world (UK, US and Europe), working to Covid-19 restrictions.

WORLD MEDIA RIGHTS, *Assistant Producer*, **Road to Victory (Netflix)**, June 29th – September 4th 2020
Reference: [excised]
I researched two episodes in the series ('Battle for Berlin' and 'Battle of the Philippine Sea'), and set up interview shoots, working around Covid-19 restrictions. I also sourced archive and pulled sync for the edit.

BROOK LAPPING, *Assistant Producer*, **Sound of TV (BBC Four)**, January 6th – March 13th 2020
Reference: [excised]
I set up interview shoots in the UK and US, and researched and wrote the production script for Episode 2.

TALESMITH, *Development Producer*, **Earth Rise S12 (Al Jazeera)**, November 4th – 29th 2019
Reference: [excised]
I developed the stories for all six episodes of Series 12 of Earth Rise, working with presenters and organisations across the globe to tell the stories of innovative environmental solutions.

BLINK FILMS, *Drama Producer*, **Treasures Decoded S6 (Channel 5/ Smithsonian/BBC Worldwide)**, April 29th – June 22nd 2019
Reference: [excised]
I set up two weeks of drama reconstruction filming at a London-based studio, working closely with casting agencies, and took on the role of 2nd AD during the shoot.

VARIOUS RESEARCHER AND AP ROLES, 2015–2018
Please email me if you would like further details of these roles, or see my Talent Manager profile.

Independent Projects

PAINTING FREEDOM, *Producer/Director*
https://vimeo.com/273480896
Over the course of a year I developed, directed, shot and produced a documentary about an art workshop run by British artist Hannah Rose Thomas with a group of Yazidi women who had escaped ISIS captivity. The film won Best International Documentary at the 300 Seconds Film Festival.

AGAINST THE LORE PODCAST, *Host*
https://anchor.fm/againstthelore
In 2021 I launched Against the Lore, an ancient history podcast designed to make classics accessible to those who didn't have the opportunity to study it at school. I am the resident expert on Roman history, and I manage the podcast together with the other three hosts.

Qualifications

Classics BA Hons (Durham)	2:1
Strategic Communications MA (King's College London)	Distinction

Quiz: which genre should I choose?

Factual TV covers many different genres under its umbrella. Sometimes Factual TV is also called 'unscripted' – which is misleading because there is always a script. It's called unscripted to differentiate it from 'scripted' television, which is essentially drama. This is why 'factual' is a better term – it's television about subject matter that's really happening, rather than what has come out of a writer's imagination.

Below is a rundown of some of the genres covered by Factual TV. Sometimes these genres overlap slightly; sometimes shows within the same genre will have very different tones and audiences.

- **Current affairs**
  Think *Newsnight*, *Panorama*, *Dispatches*. Current affairs shows draw heavily on broadcast journalism but offer a deeper dive into news topics. They may involve sensitive access or delve into hard-hitting, unpleasant stories.

- **Observational documentaries**
  These are shows that offer an insight into how people live, or how an organisation works. They include series such as *24 Hours in A&E*, *Ambulance* or *Emma Willis: Delivering Babies*. They usually involve a lot of setup, including building the relationship with the participating organisation, then very intense shoots over a limited period of time.

- **Specialist factual**
  These shows are usually extra-curricular educational, but for grown-ups. You'll need at least a Bachelor's degree to work on

these, either in science or history. Those two topics make up the bread and butter of specialist factual programming, although you'll also get shows that cover engineering and even music.

- Travel
  One of the wonderful things about television is that it brings the world into your living room. Someone who may not be able to afford a three-week trip to Japan can settle down to watch Joanna Lumley gliding through Tokyo and pretending to like pickled octopus. These shows rely heavily on the presenter and will usually have an element of formatting – whether that's a comedic component, watching someone out of their comfort zone, a mission of discovery or character development.

- Format & game
  These shows are defined by a set of rules or challenges. *Love Island*, *Naked Attraction*, *The Great British Bake Off* and *Pointless* all fall into this category. Most comedy shows are also format shows – think *8 out of 10 Cats*, *Have I Got News for You*, *Would I Lie to You?* They all follow a set format. These shows rely heavily on good casting and sometimes even recruit specialist question writers. They also pay well (a successful format can make a production company millions) and are designed to be repeatable, which means if you do well, you will have guaranteed work on multiple series of the same show.

- Studio & live
  These can sometimes involve challenges, like format shows, but usually are based on interactions between celebrity guests within a studio setting, such as *Good Morning Britain*, *The Graham Norton Show* or *The One Show* (which is also classified as a magazine show). They involve a lot of preparation and run to a tight schedule, but once it's done, it's done, which can help if you like to compartmentalise your work.

Not sure if you want to work in current affairs docs, travel shows, format shows, studio shows or specialist factual? One way to decide is to try lots of different jobs on different shows, but if you'd rather get a head start, this quiz should help you work out which genre you're best suited to.

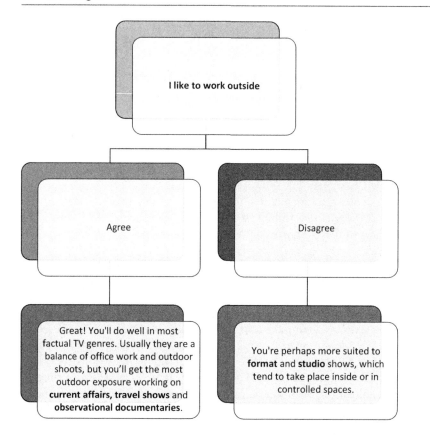

I like to work outside

Agree

Disagree

Great! You'll do well in most factual TV genres. Usually they are a balance of office work and outdoor shoots, but you'll get the most outdoor exposure working on **current affairs, travel shows** and **observational documentaries**.

You're perhaps more suited to **format** and **studio** shows, which tend to take place inside or in controlled spaces.

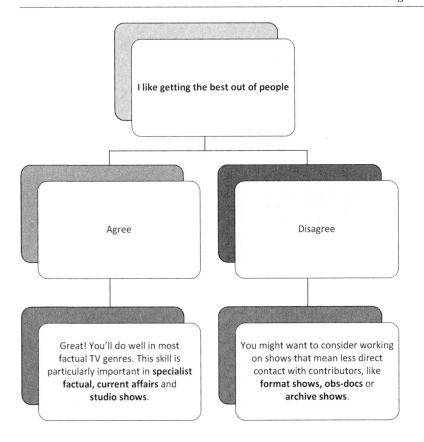

I like getting the best out of people

Agree

Disagree

Great! You'll do well in most factual TV genres. This skill is particularly important in **specialist factual, current affairs** and **studio shows**.

You might want to consider working on shows that mean less direct contact with contributors, like **format shows, obs-docs** or **archive shows**.

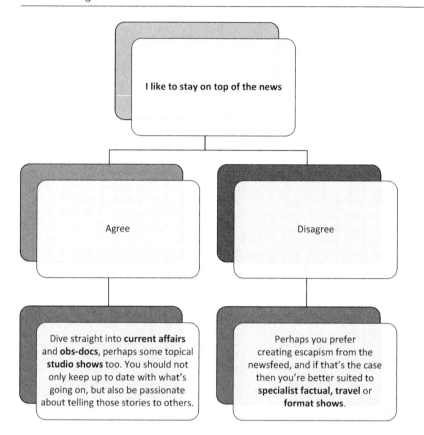

I like to stay on top of the news

Agree

Disagree

Dive straight into **current affairs** and **obs-docs**, perhaps some topical **studio shows** too. You should not only keep up to date with what's going on, but also be passionate about telling those stories to others.

Perhaps you prefer creating escapism from the newsfeed, and if that's the case then you're better suited to **specialist factual, travel** or **format shows**.

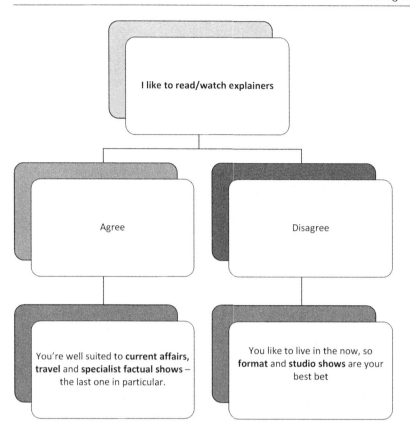

I like to read/watch explainers

Agree

Disagree

You're well suited to **current affairs, travel** and **specialist factual shows** – the last one in particular.

You like to live in the now, so **format** and **studio shows** are your best bet

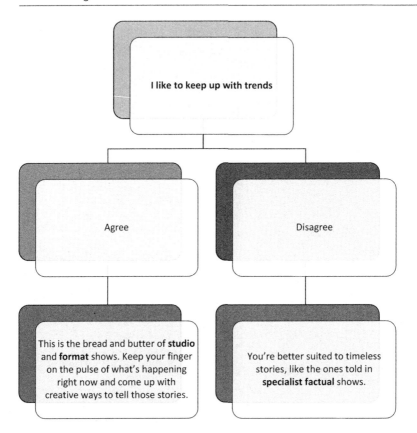

I like to keep up with trends

Agree

Disagree

This is the bread and butter of **studio** and **format** shows. Keep your finger on the pulse of what's happening right now and come up with creative ways to tell those stories.

You're better suited to timeless stories, like the ones told in **specialist factual** shows.

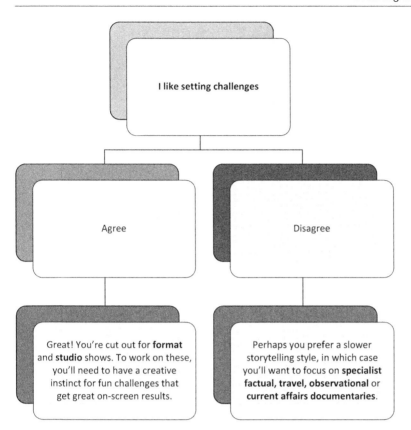

I like setting challenges

Agree

Disagree

Great! You're cut out for **format** and **studio** shows. To work on these, you'll need to have a creative instinct for fun challenges that get great on-screen results.

Perhaps you prefer a slower storytelling style, in which case you'll want to focus on **specialist factual, travel, observational** or **current affairs documentaries**.

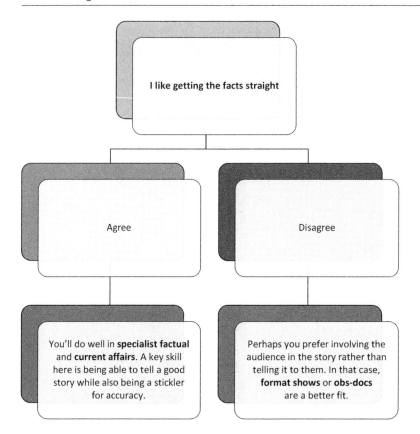

I like getting the facts straight

Agree

Disagree

You'll do well in **specialist factual** and **current affairs**. A key skill here is being able to tell a good story while also being a stickler for accuracy.

Perhaps you prefer involving the audience in the story rather than telling it to them. In that case, **format shows** or **obs-docs** are a better fit.

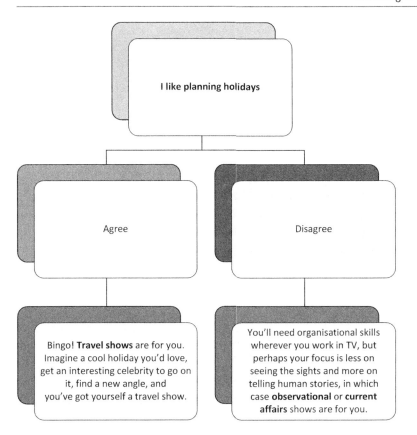

I like planning holidays

Agree

Disagree

Bingo! **Travel shows** are for you. Imagine a cool holiday you'd love, get an interesting celebrity to go on it, find a new angle, and you've got yourself a travel show.

You'll need organisational skills wherever you work in TV, but perhaps your focus is less on seeing the sights and more on telling human stories, in which case **observational** or **current affairs** shows are for you.

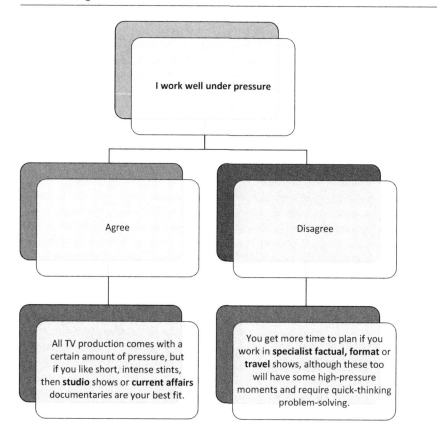

Where should I live?

The heart of the TV industry is in London. London produces content for much of Europe and the US, as well as many streaming platforms. It is the international hub of Factual TV production. That said, there are other parts of the country that specialise in certain types of programming, so if you are interested in natural history, arts or children's programming, you can forge a career in a safer city with lower rent prices. If you are just starting out and are not ready, financially or mentally, to move to London, then I would suggest focusing your energies on one of the smaller cities before making the move to the capital (see Figure 1.1).

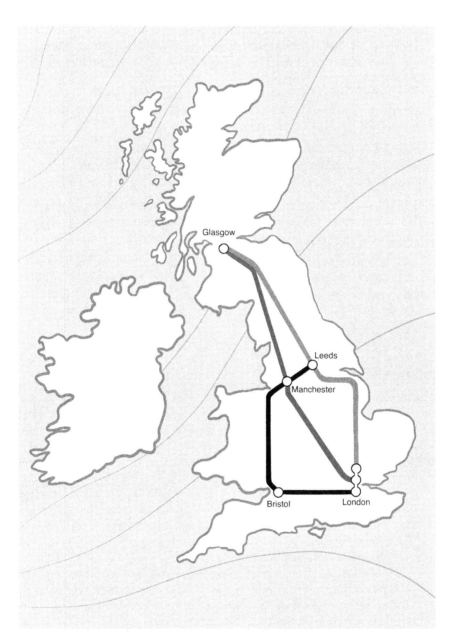

Figure 1.1 TV Hubs.

GLASGOW: there are a few production companies based here and a branch of the BBC. They mostly make arts and history programming, so if that's your cup of tea and you'd rather not live in London, head to Glasgow.

MANCHESTER: this is where you want to be for children's programming, sports and big studio shows. MediaCity in Salford is truly magnificent.

LEEDS: Channel 4 is now based here, as are several production companies that specialise in cutting-edge, gritty current affairs documentaries. If that's your jam, focus your energies here.

BRISTOL: if you love natural history, you'll want to base yourself here. This is where the BBC's Natural History Unit is located, along with several other production companies that have sprung up around it.

LONDON: for everything else, there's London. You'll still get arts, history and current affairs documentaries being made here, as well as natural history and studio shows. It's more competitive as there's a larger community, but equally there are many more options and opportunities here.

Encouragement

Starting out in television is hard. Most people in the industry remember this and will be happy to help if you approach them politely. Try to stay proactive and open-minded as you work your way into and then through the industry. If it is any consolation, this is the blog I wrote when I first started – the blog that eventually led to this book.

> I started lucky. My many student holiday jobs as an unpaid runner meant that I managed to get myself a position as a Junior Researcher on Mary Beard's new series, *Meet the Roman Empire*, straight after Finals. Well, Junior Researcher was a bit of a misnomer – I was their only researcher. It was steady work for nearly three months.
>
> And then my contract ended. Despite promises of working on other TV series with the same company, either the budget or the circumstances fell through. So I got myself an internship with ITN, and an internship with Bettany Hughes, another Classics presenter.
>
> Then ITN announced at the end of my internship that they didn't actually have a researcher position. So I got a pub job. Or two. It just about paid the rent; the tips paid for my food.

Then I went to a free launch night of a women's film festival and made a friend. She got me a day's runner work, which was amazing, and, after a month of pub work, made me remember how much I love TV!

But that was just one day. Then I went to support my friend at a stand-up gig, and there I met a guy who worked for a comedy production company. I got another internship. Still unpaid. Still juggling pub work alongside it.

So you meet me now, pretty skint, working two pub jobs, having applied for jobs in TV every day for several months. A CV that's covered in As and A*s, a long list of qualifications and work experience placements, links to documentaries and films I've made. To be honest, it really couldn't be much shinier. But apparently 'this is how TV works'.

Yeah, it's an unforgiving industry, based almost solely in a city that is very unforgiving: expensive, busy, and sometimes dangerous. No one goes into TV for the money or the stability. But as long as we remember why we started working in it, we remember why it's all worth it.

Summary

- Network, network, network
- Apply for TV entry schemes
- Format your CV correctly
- Think tactically: work out which genre is for you and where you want to live. Focus your energy there.

What to watch

Watch a full day's programming on a broadcasting channel (a great exercise for a duvet day). Take notes on the different types of shows that are broadcast, which categories they fall into and what times they are broadcast. Watch the credits to find out which production companies made them. This will give you an understanding of the range of content made for TV, who makes it and which audience they're targeting with each show.

Chapter 2

Working as a team

This chapter will prepare you for what to expect on your first day in the office – who else will be there, what they each do and where those roles overlap. TV is very hierarchical, so it's important to distinguish the big cheeses from the work wives – and most importantly, who will be able to help you set up your new email address or show you where the stationery cupboard is.

The exact balance of the production team will vary depending on the type of production and the budget, but as a rule, these are the characters you should look out for in your team. The roles are divided into two categories: editorial and production. Editorial roles cover the structure and narrative of the show or series; production roles cover the practical aspects of budget management and logistics. This book is designed to support an editorial career in Factual TV, but I've included a brief section in this chapter on what you can expect from a career in production. These are the characters you should look out for in your team (see Table 2.1).

Editorial

- **EXECUTIVE PRODUCER**
  If you are at entry level, you won't have much contact with the exec. They will be working across a few different projects and are responsible for liaising with the commissioner about the overall direction of the show/series. They will make final decisions on any issues that affect the whole show.

- **SERIES PRODUCER**
  They are responsible for overseeing the day-to-day progress of the production. They will have final say on any stylistic decisions as well as sign-off on large costs.

DOI: 10.4324/9781003294009-3

- **DIRECTOR**

  Depending on the number of episodes being made, there may be more than one director working on the project. They are responsible for the scriptwriting, storytelling, visual aesthetic and structure of the programmes.

- **PRODUCER/ASSISTANT PRODUCER**

  A production will likely have either of these but rarely both. A producer works with the director to oversee the smooth running of the production as a whole and has more say over budget allowances and editorial direction. The assistant producer (AP) (confusingly) assists the director(s), helping with research for the script, casting choices or liaising on production logistics with the production manager (PM). For example, if a filming location is required, the AP will liaise with the director to determine what sort of location is required to fulfil the storytelling needs of the production, then work with the PM to find something that fits both the editorial requirements and the budget constraints. The AP might be the one to book the location, but the PM will pay for it.

- **RESEARCHER**

  Even if there are multiple teams of directors and APs, there will usually be just one researcher across a series. They are responsible for … well … research, and supplying that research to the directors to inform their scripts. Researchers may also help with some of the logistics.

- **RUNNER**

  The runner answers to everyone – production and editorial. They will run errands – getting supplies, keeping everyone suitably fed and watered, helping the researcher or helping with filming.

Working with production (from the editorial perspective)

The relationship between editorial and production should be one founded on deep mutual respect. Everyone is working together for the same goal: to make the show the best it possibly can be with the resources available. The production team will do their best to make sure the editorial team get what they need for the production as long as the editorial team keep their demands within the bounds of reason. Equally, the editorial team should treat a budget seriously and use their creative skills to keep their demands within the parameters set by the budget. I have always maintained good

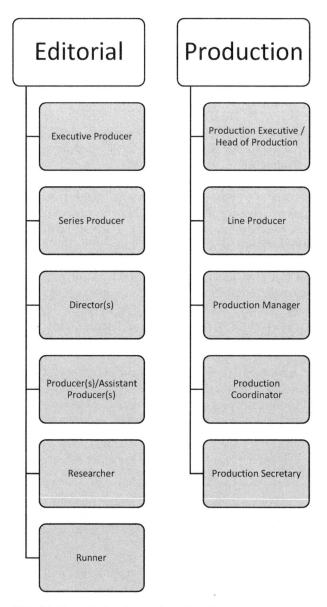

Table 2.1 Organisational chart for editorial and production

relationships with production teams, offering to help them wherever possible, but have stopped short of budget decisions when they were not mine to make, respecting the authority of the production team on that matter.

Production

Interview with Production Manager Juliet (Jules) Walker

The career path in production generally starts with an entry-level position such as runner, production secretary or production assistant, then progresses to production coordinator (PC), after which you will look to be a production manager/line producer and finally a production executive.

Entry-level jobs can be challenging with many varied responsibilities that need juggling to keep everyone happy. These can range from grabbing lunch, research, reconciling floats, monitoring and ordering office and stationery supplies, making tea/coffee ... the list is vast!

Production can be a fast-paced environment. Things change constantly – you will need to be even more prepared and organised than you can imagine. A lot of time and energy in production is spent rescheduling and reorganising existing plans. Natural problem-solvers and organisers thrive in this environment. If you make a great impression in this role, the company will want to invest in you to grow your skills and progress to become a PC and on to a PM and beyond. Starting at entry level is a great way to watch and learn how production works. Be friendly and inquisitive – if you are helpful to people they will want to share their knowledge, which will enable you to understand how the department runs and where best to direct your help and resources.

The production department have great camaraderie, they help keep morale high and provide much-needed reassurance along the way. If you thrive in high-pressured roles, you'll love the unpredictable but rewarding career offered in a production role.

- **LINE PRODUCER/PRODUCTION EXECUTIVE**
  Larger productions tend to have a line producer who oversees the budget, production schedule, forecasting, logistics and insurance of the whole show. They may be working across multiple projects. If there is no line producer, the overall responsibility may fall to the production executive, who oversees the production aspects for every production at the company. They are very busy and work alongside the executive producers or head of production.

- **PRODUCTION MANAGER**
  The PM is your go-to for your contract, any questions concerning budget, schedule and logistics – and, unofficially, your wellbeing. TV production companies rarely have an HR department, so the responsibility for the safety and health of every member of the production team tends to fall to the PM. While this tends to be an office-based role (the production team rarely go on shoots), the

PM will need to be on standby whenever a team is out on a shoot, as they will be the person the director or producer calls if they run into a problem that cannot be solved on the ground. This requires a cool head, quick thinking, the ability to prioritise and a willingness to answer calls late at night/early in the morning.

- **PRODUCTION COORDINATOR**
  The PC assists the PM. They cover all of the admin crucial to the smooth running of a production. This may include creating the call sheet, assigning and reconciling floats, handling hotel and travel bookings and cost manager software, among other day-to-day organisational requests. They may be working on one production or across several.

- **PRODUCTION SECRETARY**
  The production secretary is another support role, reporting to the PM. The production secretary will be required to cover various tasks, including anything from opening and distributing post to typing scripts/photocopying. It's a great entry-level position that offers the potential to gain wide-ranging knowledge of how production works. Smile, ask lots of questions and people will be happy to share their knowledge and experience.

Working with editorial (from the production perspective): interview with Juliet (Jules) Walker

The role of production is to keep the production on schedule, to budget and delivered on time. The production team need to be organised and across all aspects of what's needed for the show. Production is there to meet the practical and everyday requirements, such as accommodation and transport, as well as keeping track of paperwork and ensuring everything runs safely.

Editorial want to make the best film they possibly can, so this can be a difficult balance and needs to be managed carefully and collaboratively.

Production can often feel the editorial team are throwing things at them whimsically without much thought or planning, which can be frustrating and not always achievable. Sometimes a permit may be needed for a location, or a prop may have a few days' lead time to obtain. The earlier any requests can be given to the production team, the better. Tight deadlines and last-minute requests can be the downfall of a shoot, not to mention putting safety considerations at risk.

For example, if there is shoot that involves outdoor filming, it will likely be a beautiful location where the director will want to (understandably) film during the golden hour, which in summer months can be very early morning or quite late into the evening. Production would need to consider where the location is, if the crew can travel and shoot everything needed from that location in the time allocated, while also allowing for rest time. Will overnights be required? Will a longer day result in overtime? If so, can a deal be done with the crew to keep within the allocated budget and most importantly avoid long shoot/travel days to keep the crew safe from fatigue? It seems so minor to 'just want to film' at a certain time but there can be a lot of considerations around what seems to be a minor request.

The director is responsible for telling a story visually: they will often ask for a unicorn when the budget will only allow for a donkey with a traffic cone! The challenge is to collaboratively meet somewhere in the middle with regards to budget and what can be achieved. Not all donkeys are available at short notice! Whatever the resolution, it is very likely to require give and take on both sides. Often a director can be bullish about what they want to do and how they want things to be, but there's always a solution or compromise. It's important to be open and collaborative, but it also takes strength and confidence to push back and help find a solution that both editorial and production are happy with. The phrase 'firm but fair' comes into play here, one I have mastered over the years!

Editorial will always want more time: more time to shoot and more time to edit. However, the budget is finite and therefore keeping to the schedule is imperative. Again, our favourite word 'collaborate' comes in handy. Often there will need to be give and take – for example, can the director live without a music composer and use library music to shift some of the budget around? It's always prudent to follow up with the team in writing to ensure everyone is aware of any schedule and/or budget changes.

Production teams plan, schedule, troubleshoot and problem-solve. They run the budget and ensure everyone is working safely. They are the gear box of the car that gets the film from A to B. So remember to say thank you and ask how they are rather than jumping straight in with 'where's my unicorn'! Ultimately, we're all on the same production journey and we all want the best film possible. So play nice, be kind and respect the role of each member of the team. Productions are like boulders: they don't move on their own but if we all participate together, that boulder will roll!

SUMMARY

- Respect your other team members and their roles
- Know the hierarchy
- Make friends with everyone on the team

Chapter 3

Runner

Welcome to stage one! Most people start out in TV as runners. If you have a relevant degree, you may be able to skip straight to researcher level, but even then, it's a good idea to get some experience as a runner so you know what life is like on set.

How to get a runner job

There are three main ways to get a runner job:

1. Join the Runners' Facebook group. Search 'People in TV: Runners'.
2. Send your CV to your network, making it clear you're available for runner jobs
3. Send your CV to production companies that produce shows that need runners

The most important skill you can have as a runner is a proactive, positive attitude. However, there are a couple of other skills that will work to your advantage. If you have a clean driving licence, make sure you mention that in your application email or at the top of your CV. Likewise with first aid training. Another important skill is making a good cup of tea or coffee – this is probably the skill you'll use most often. I drink coffee, but not tea – as a result I was always praised for my 'rocket fuel' coffee, but slated for the weak teas I would bring people on set. Make sure you know how to stew a builder's brew.

There's no one-size-fits-all for runner jobs. Each one will be different, with new challenges, new personalities, new responsibilities and new demands. But before we go into the specifics of the three main types of runner, here are a few golden rules that apply across any job:

DOI: 10.4324/9781003294009-4

Golden rules

- Take every opportunity and learn from it
- Be keen and helpful and liked
- Keep in contact with people you meet
- Whatever job you get, be the best at it
- You are only as good as your last job. This means three things:
  - Recruiters will rarely look beyond the latest credit on your CV
  - You should upgrade with each job
  - You last job will probably help you get your next one – if you use your network correctly
- Get fit – muscles and stamina help on set!
- Always be early or on time, never, ever late
- Never assume – if you are unsure, ask
- Don't be on your phone all the time. Unless you've been asked to look something up or contact someone, you should be alert and ready to take instructions.
- Don't sit down. If you do need to sit, perch or lean. You need to be ready to go at any given moment. Personally, I don't like this rule – I think if you don't have a job to do at that moment, you should be able to sit down. However, some people in television with an older mindset don't like to see runners sitting.

What to wear

- A good pair of shoes. Either comfy waterproof trainers or prefer-ably lace-up, military-style boots. You shouldn't need steel toe cap boots, and if you do, the production company should supply these.
- Warm layers. If you're on a shoot, you will likely be out and about. The weather can be unpredictable (especially in the UK). Make sure you have a hat, gloves, waterproof, thermals – the lot.
- Trousers with pockets. For men, this is a no-brainer, but women's trousers don't always have pockets. Make sure you have a prac-tical pair with pockets. Jeans are fine, but I've always found walking or cargo trousers to be more practical. Leggings are a big no-no, especially as they don't support a radio should you need to clip one to your belt or waistband.
- A bum bag (US: fanny pack). You'll need to keep a lot of items within easy access. Your pockets may not be able to hold every-thing. A bum bag is therefore very useful, especially as you don't want to keep swinging your rucksack off your shoulder every time you need something.

Office runner

This is the holy grail of runner jobs and therefore highly competitive! The office runner usually acts as a receptionist, performs inductions for new staff, keeps the office supplied with stationery, milk, coffee, tea and whatever else is required, organises office-wide events and is often recruited to help out on productions. Everyone knows the office runner, and they know everyone, which makes office running the ideal position for networking and moving through to a production.

Let's hear more about what is involved with office running, and how to get those coveted jobs, from Will Taylor-Gammon.

Interview with Will Taylor-Gammon

To get an office runner job, you need to show that you have a sincere interest in Factual TV. My journalism degree definitely helped, as I was able to display an interest in Factual TV by highlighting my passion for researching and writing about real-life stories. In interviews and in my cover letter I also discussed specific modules I had learned like News Video Reporting, which I knew would help bridge the gap between journalism and video production/TV by showing my enthusiasm for visual storytelling.

TV jobs are renowned for being very competitive, so to get the job you have to show that you are willing to go above and beyond most other people, which means thinking outside of the box. For weeks and weeks I was on Facebook groups advertising my CV, reading tips on how to get a job and be a good runner, taking free courses and bolstering my CV as much as possible.

I managed to work on a couple of shoots as a runner. One was an advert and another was a small recording of a dancer. I also volunteered at a local film festival. Working on the shoots and at the film festival showed that I was genuinely interested and had actively taken steps to pursue a career in production. For my application I focused on these experiences and the skills I had learned (like handling petty cash) to persuade the employer that not only did I have a passion for TV, but that I already had the experience and skills they were looking for, and that I could perform the duties that were expected of me. I also had previous experience working as a kitchen runner/waiter for a few months. These people-facing jobs provided great transferable skills that were really useful in my application stage. Eventually, I got my job through a scheme, so I would highly recommend looking at and applying for schemes, jobs boards and employers who are willing to invest in new talent.

It is also worthwhile researching the company you are applying for, which can mean watching a few episodes of their shows, and seeing what productions they might have in the pipeline. You can then talk about this in your cover letter and interview, as this shows you actually care about the content they make.

The main task for the office runner is to help the office manager and support them with any task in ensuring that the office runs smoothly, so that productions can get on with their work efficiently and create fantastic TV. Therefore, the key responsibilities of an office runner are incredibly varied. It could be something as simple as making cups of tea and coffee, especially for guests and external meetings, keeping the office clean and tidy, and restocking the kitchen and stationery cupboards. For my first two weeks, the dishwasher had broken, so I spent most of my time washing up. These responsibilities can seem quite tedious but are crucial to the running of the office. People quickly turn when there isn't any milk for their tea!

Other responsibilities include being the face of the company, so greeting guests when they arrive and handling incoming calls and general mailboxes, taking messages and forging good relationships to develop a positive office culture, which is needed in an environment that can quickly turn stressful for a production team. You can also find yourself with higher-pressure duties, like being a keyholder and opening/closing the office, reconciling the office float, setting up new employees with IT accounts, handling confidential documents, and many more *ad hoc* tasks.

Introducing yourself is key to networking. In my first week, my manager gave me a box of chocolates, and told me to go round to every team, introduce myself and ask people some questions (as long as they were not too busy). Doing this was a brilliant way to get myself familiar with all the productions going on, have people remember me from the start, and put down those roots in the company as someone who is friendly and wants to chat. Having those conversations early on made me stand out as someone who was interested in the industry and passionate about learning more and networking. So, I would highly recommend grabbing a box of chocolates, going round each team and introducing yourself.

If possible, try to go to every social event. If it is a wrap party, leaving drinks or a Friday after-work social, try and go to it. There will be lots of opportunities to talk to people, especially external people who do not directly work for the company. In these situations, you can ask a lot of questions and not be worried about making someone miss any deadlines or work that they need to do. When you ask a lot of questions, you portray yourself as someone who is curious and interested, and that will make someone think that you are sincerely passionate, and they will consider you when future opportunities arise. I did exactly this at a wrap party and managed to speak to a director. A few weeks later, I then shadowed that director for a couple of days.

The best way to get involved with productions is by saying yes to everything. Obviously, you need to make sure your workload is managed, as all the tasks can quickly pile up, but by saying yes, you are proving yourself as someone who is able to take any task that gets thrown at them. This can then translate to productions giving you more work. Initially, I sent an email to the 'Everyone' mail group, saying that I would be happy to help anyone if they had an issue or some work that needed to be done. Within a month I was helping with editing reels, researching for a show, transcribing, and much more.

Also, approach production teams directly. You can put out an email asking if anyone needs a hand with some work, but sometimes this method does not get a response. I found it more effective to go up to an assistant producer (AP)/researcher or junior production manager/production coordinator (PC) and ask if there was anything they needed help with. People can sometimes think you are just being nice, but as I was actively going to people and asking if they needed assistance, they saw that I was free and up to the task, and so they would be more than happy to give me production work to do. Once a production gives you some work, and you complete the task well, you will then find them giving you more responsibility. For example, I helped one production by moving some props from one location to another. A month later, I was helping to take care of high-profile talent on a shoot.

The best way to leverage your position to step up is to show your hard work and the ways in which you have benefited the company. Projects might get commissioned and so it is good to look for openings and opportunities that can take you to the next level, and when you apply, focus on the skills and the experience they are looking for. Don't just tell the hiring employer what you have done, but show how it helped a production. For example, providing additional research for a production is great, but then demonstrating that the information you found later helped the casting team will make you stand out and prove how much you benefited the team.

Networking can also help, as those friendly relationships you have been building can help you get that future position. It might be a conversation you have had with a producer about being interested in going the editorial route with your career that makes them think of you for the job. Or it might be that you have a friend who sees an opportunity open up for you.

Ultimately, your hard work and friendliness will naturally cause you to excel and provide proof that you are deserving of that next-level role.

Studio runner

A studio runner is usually on location within the studio setting. They are responsible for looking after the talent, such as the presenter, cast, guests, panellists, participants or interviewees, as well as supplying refreshments and food. Let's hear more about what it takes to be a great studio runner from Mitch Langcaster-James.

Interview with Mitch Langcaster-James

TV can be made in so many different spaces, whether you're interviewing the general public on the street, or filming an award ceremony in a theatre. But for me, nothing feels more like making television than being in a traditional TV studio. Shows filmed in studios are often referred to as 'shiny floor shows', which refers to the physical floor, which is traditionally covered in a glossy, plastic overlay. Talent shows, game shows and chat shows are just a few of the kinds of programmes usually filmed in similar shiny-floor studios, all of which will need runners. Runners are the backbone of a TV show; if runners didn't exist, it would be incredibly difficult to make TV. Back when I first started my career in TV, my first job – as it is for most people in the industry – was as a runner and it's seen as a real rite of passage.

Anyone can become a studio runner. To start with, you need the basic qualities of any good runner – being punctual, reliable, quick and friendly. There are then a number of ways to get this specific role. Some studios have their own in-house runners, who help run the day-to-day of the studio itself, as opposed to working on a specific production. This can be a great way to meet lots of different producers and production managers, from a mix of production companies, all of whom might be able to help you get a job on an actual show. Personally, I went down a slightly different route. I found that back when I was starting out, it was often easier to get work regionally, where there was less competition. When I was studying at university in the North-East I would contact production companies and see if they needed any help locally. Lots of shows would pass through the North-East, even if just for a day or two, shooting a VT [a short film insert], on a casting tour or on the hunt for a filming location. I'd been picking up runner work for a few months when I was asked to help out with the casting of a new quiz show, which was travelling around the country looking for regional contestants. As a runner, and even when you become more senior, you're only ever as good as your last job, so it's important to always try to impress. Fortunately for me, this quiz show was then returning to London after the casting tour to film at a major TV studio. As I'd worked with them before and already started to form a relationship with the contestants, I was asked to come down to London for the studio record of the show.

Being a runner on a studio show isn't easy, as it's one of the most varied roles you can do and comes with high expectations. For example, you need to have the people skills to be meeting and looking after high-profile guests, but have the organisational skills to understand the printing and distribution of scripts. One of my early studio runner roles was on a high-profile celebrity game show. One minute I'd be serving drinks to the well-known guests (referred to as 'talent'), the next minute taking out the trash and then before I knew it, I'd be on set being filmed dressed up as a tickle monster as part of a game! Versatility really is key.

The great thing about studio shows it that they usually have similar systems and infrastructures in place: an on-site production office, a gallery for the director and editorial team, even catering facilities. Once you've worked on one studio show, it typically gets easier and easier, as you get used to their general way of operating, the terminology used and who does what role. It also becomes easier as you begin to work your way round the different major studios. Television Centre, Pinewood, Elstree – all major studios you will likely encounter throughout your career, and when you've worked there once, it starts to become second nature. That being said, we all have to start somewhere, so your first day as a studio runner can be a big one.

Let's say you've managed to get your first day as a studio runner. Congratulations! Before turning up on your first day, clarify exactly what it is they'd like you to wear. As the runner, you'll often be the person who is running in and out of every part of the studio the most, so you'll usually be asked to wear 'studio blacks', which, as you can imagine, means head-to-toe black. That way, if you accidentally walk through the back of shot, or you're working on the studio floor, you still won't be seen.

If you've never worked in a studio before, chances are you may also have not had to communicate over a radio yet, usually referred to as 'comms'. Although the equipment can vary slightly, the general etiquette is the same. Firstly, find out from the production team which channels are for which teams; you don't want to accidentally be telling the director all about the paper delivery that has just arrived! Always start by stating who you are and who the person is you're hoping to speak to – for example, 'Mitch to Jasmine' – and then wait for them to acknowledge you before carrying on. Keep communication concise and clear, and remember you never know who's listening, so only share what you're happy for everyone to know.

When I was starting out as a studio runner and joining a new show, especially if it was my first time in that studio, I would get in as early as possible on my first day and get acquainted with where everything is. As the runner, you want to know your way around the studio like the back of your hand. If someone calls for you over comms and asks you to run some scripts from the production office up to the gallery, you need to know the absolute quickest route to get them there. Also keep in mind that when you actually start shooting, the studio itself will be very dark and you want to know exactly what door leads where before filming begins. Sometimes studios can feel like a maze – some of them actually are! But with time you'll get to know them all, and never be too afraid to ask for help or directions.

Naturally, job responsibilities can vary from show to show, but as a studio runner, there are a few key tasks you're typically across. As with most runner roles, you're often required to keep everyone fed and watered. It might not always feel like the most glamorous task, but bringing people tea and coffee can be a great way to get your face out there and get chatting to more senior members of the team. You'll regularly find that your director, executive producer, script supervisor, maybe even graphics team, lighting director and more, will be based in galleries, sitting in the same seats throughout production. Top tip, draw yourself a little layout of the gallery and label each seat with the person's name, their job role, their tea or coffee preferences and any other notes that might be relevant. For example, someone might come running up to you and ask you to sprint a tea up to 'Simon', because he was stuck in traffic and has arrived late. In that scenario, you want to know who Simon is, exactly where he sits and how he takes his tea. The fact that you've also noted down he asked you for an almond croissant the week before – so you drop one off unrequested with the tea – might make his day and highlights your attention to detail.

Studio runner roles can often require you to be both creative and very organised. It might be that you're out buying props that will be used in a game, briefing contestants or helping to decorate the set. However, you will likely also be expected to be across making lanyards, giving access lists to security or putting signs up to help direct people to where they need to be. In the lead-up to a studio record day, the editorial team will also typically have been working on scripts for the presenters, as well as overseeing running orders, which are documents that keep track of exactly what is happening in each section of the show and help keep things running to time. A Studio runner is often tasked with making sure these are all printed, stapled and distributed to all the right people ahead of the show. It may sound simple, but when there's been a script change and they all have to be reprinted but the photocopier has died, it can be incredibly stressful. As early as you can, find out exactly who will need what paperwork and if the show has any systems in place. For example, if you're filming multiple episodes in a week, it may be that the production team want you to alternate the colour of paper you use for each record. That way it's harder for people to accidentally end up working off the wrong script and makes it easier for you to know which paperwork is out of date.

You'll often hear people in TV say it's all about 'who you know', which can in some instances be true. Networking is an important part of working in the TV industry but it's crucial to know the right time and place. If it's 30 seconds before you go live on a daytime talk show, asking the director if you can shadow him at work is not going to do you any favours. If you've got a Hollywood actor in the studio and you ask for their phone number in the hopes they can get you work on another TV show, that's not networking, it's being unprofessional. However, if your PC has a spare 15 minutes, politely mentioning you'd love to look at becoming a Production Secretary in the future, and asking if they wouldn't mind talking to you about it, is absolutely fine. Similarly, if you end up sitting opposite an AP over lunch and they ask you what your aims are, be honest and ask for advice. At some point we all started as runners, so most people are happy to help.

Let's say you've been working as a runner for a little while, you've been working consistently and you've started to build a network of people around you, which is brilliant. You've become friendly with some members of the editorial team and picked their brains about becoming a researcher and you want to know what it takes to make that jump. The hardest thing about stepping up in any role, whether it be runner to researcher or runner to production secretary, is that you need someone to take a chance on you. You need a senior member of the show to trust that you're more than printing scripts, more than making tea or buying props, and that you should have more of an impact on the show itself. It's at this point that all your effort as a runner pays off; the attention to detail in bringing someone their favourite snack unrequested, the organisation of your paperwork and that amazing prop you found that no one else had even thought of. Don't underestimate those smaller tasks you do as a runner and the impact that has on people's perceptions of you. If you work hard, people will notice, and you'll be the person they think of when a position opens up.

Production runner

As a production runner, you'll likely jump from one production to the next, helping out during filming. Your duties can range from getting coffees for people, to holding a reflector, to distributing heat packs, to making sure the director drinks enough water, to looking after a presenter, to buying props, to ensuring continuity of wood shavings between takes (this was genuinely something I did once). The length of contract could range from a single day to several weeks. On a single day shoot, it's harder to form strong friendships and connections with the rest of the crew, but equally over the course of several weeks it's harder to keep up the same level of energy. That said, you will do well if you make a good impression and form friendships on your single day shoot and if you maintain a peppy demeanour throughout the longer shoots.

Here are three important things to know before you start your first Runner job:

- **Money**
  It is likely you will be entrusted with a 'float', money used for buying food, drinks and whatever else the production needs. This will be provided by the production manager (PM) or PC and should be returned to them at the end of the day. You should have a clear plastic wallet handy in which to keep the money, along with receipts for all your purchases. You must keep the receipts

as they get balanced against the remaining money in the float: if there is a discrepancy, the production company usually reserves the right to take this off your pay.

- **Call sheet**
  Before the start of the production (sometimes just the night before, often late the night before) you will be sent a call sheet. You must have a copy on you at all times – if you have access to a printer, make sure you print more than one copy. The talent inevitably forgets their copy of the call sheet, so it's an instant win for you if you can provide them with one. You must read the call sheet as it contains all the important information about the shoot, including who else will be there, emergency contacts and the shooting schedule. You don't need to memorise all the information, but you should be familiar with important details such as the nearest parking to the shooting location, the nearest hospital and nearby eateries/restaurants. The night before the shoot, you should plug the key contacts into your phone, so that you can easily reach them in case of a query or emergency.

- **Hierarchy**
  Television is a very hierarchical industry that contains many individuals who are sensitive about their position in the hierarchy. You can use the call sheet to find out who will be on the shoot and what their roles are. Of course, you should be respectful to everyone on set, but particularly the core editorial team, such as the director and producer. Knowing the hierarchy can also help you to prioritise any demands made of you during the shoot. Requests from the talent must be your top priority, followed by the production team, followed by the crew – unless those are demands for sustenance, in which case the priority list is talent, crew, production. A fed team is a happy team. If you are unsure about how to carry out a request, make sure you ask for clarification. Even if this incites an annoyed comeback, it is certainly preferable to carrying out the task incorrectly, which could have serious consequences for the production.

As you prepare for your first runner job, make sure you pack an appropriate bag with all the things you'll need for the shoot. Your bag should be sturdy and waterproof, with room for all of the following things:

Run bag checklist

- Utility knife (e.g. Swiss Army knife)
- Clear pencil case or folder, for money
- Gaffa tape/electrical tape
- Tissues
- First aid kit
- Bottle of water
- Notebook and pen
- Call sheet and script
- Basic make-up (translucent powder and application sponge or brush) – for the talent. Yes, lads, you should pack this too.
- Chewing gum
- Props/costumes/any additional items you've been asked to bring

Call sheet

I've mentioned the call sheet a couple of times now – it is the single most important document on a shoot. At runner level, you only need to know how to read one, not write one – it's the production team's job to write and send the call sheet. See Table 3.1 for an example of how a typical call sheet is laid out, so you know how to find important information should you need it.

Table 3.1 Example call sheet

SERIES NAME AND NUMBER **Filming subject** Filming dates
TECH SPEC
PICTURE: **Aspect Ratio 16:9 HD** **1080p 29.97 NTSC Progressive** **Slog 3**
TAPE LABELS
Next Roll Number: SERIES_CODE_CAMERA NUMBER_ROLL NUMBER_ YYMMDD N.B Please ensure you put the **ROLL NUMBER, DATE, STORY, LOCATION &** **DESCRIPTION** on your log for reference

CREW ON LOCATION		
ROLE	NAME	CONTACT DETAILS
ROLE	NAME	CONTACT DETAILS

CONTRIBUTORS/LOCATIONS AND CONTACT DETAILS		
LOCATION & DATE	NAME	CONTACT DETAILS

CAR HIRE			
INFO	DRIVERS	DATE / TIME	ACCOUNT INFO

ACCOMMODATION			
ACCOMMODATION	GUESTS	DATES	INFO

EMERGENCY CONTACTS		
LOCATION		
NEAREST HOSPITAL (EMERGENCY ROOM)	ADDRESS	PHONE NUMBER
NEAREST POLICE STATION	ADDRESS	Open 8am–8pm

INSURANCE	
Any insurance queries please get in touch with Production Manager *Certificate of Public Liability Insurance up to $10,000,000 will be in the Production Folder.*	*Contact Details for Medical Emergencies Abroad:*

HEALTH & SAFETY

The Risk Assessment for this shoot will be distributed by email with this call sheet as well as being printed and put in the team production pack. Please read it through carefully. Any concerns should be directed to your head of department.

ACCIDENT REPORTING FORMS
are in the production pack
The crew have a first aid kit

KIT	
%	

(continued)

RELEASE FORMS

ALL Release Forms:

All correspondence and documents will be sent electronically and where possible no paperwork to be handled on site. If contributors need to sign a release form on location, they will be asked to take their own pen with them

STILL PHOTOGRAPHS – DELIVERABLES

Twenty stills per episode for a series. Please see the PMD Guide in the Producer's Portal for the Unit Stills Guidelines. Image content should depict **Programme Subject Matter** (significant action scenes, talent, interviews, contributors, animals, re-enactments), **Talent** (on and off set, in posed and unposed situations, and in solo and group shots. Approved photos only), **Machinery/Equipment** (including props and other details relevant to the show), **Environment** (images illustrating geography of production location), **Making of/Behind the Scenes Digital specs:** High-resolution files are required. Use a digital SLR camera. Send the largest files your camera will produce. (Do not res down.) Files must be at least 11″ x 14″ at 300 PPI in Jpeg format.

WEATHER FORECAST

PLEASE MAKE SURE YOU PACK APPROPRIATELY FOR THE WEATHER

WK I	DATE	DATE
	Rain	Partly cloudy
TEMP:	**H:10 L:6**	**H:10 L:8**

SCHEDULE DETAILS

*** CREW TO TAKE PRODUCTION STILLS – DSLR ONLY ***
*** PLEASE PROVIDE GVs & EXTERIOR SHOTS OF EACH LOCATION ***
DATE

Sunrise: Sunset:

TIME	SCHEDULE	DETAILS

Radio etiquette

If you're a runner on studio shoots or large-scale location shoots, you will most likely be given a radio. There are rules for using them. If you've never been on radio comms before, here are some guidelines:

1. The crew will agree a common radio channel, usually Channel 1. Some departments may have sub-channels, e.g. Lighting on Channel 3. There will also be a channel allocated for longer private conversations.
2. When you're asking to speak to someone, say your name, then 'to/for', then their name. So for example, 'Zenia for Tom'.
3. If someone asks for you and you hear them, respond by saying 'Go for [your name]'. For example, 'Go for Zenia'.
4. Over-communicate. If someone asks you to do something over the radio, acknowledge them (by saying 'copy that'), complete the task, then tell them when it's done.
5. Any conversations that are longer than simple commands or questions should happen on a different channel. To do that, ask for the person you need, say the channel number you want to switch to, then switch to that channel and wait for them to come in. Don't forget to go back to Channel 1 when you're done. Even on private channels, remember to keep the conversation professional. I once discovered during a shoot that the make-up department was switching to the private channel to eavesdrop whenever they heard someone requesting a private chat on the main channel...
6. Code for the toilet is ten-one. Technically, ten-two means...well...a number two, but no one ever says that. Too much detail.
7. If you hear someone asking for you over the radio, but you're busy, just wait till you're finished and then say, 'Go again for [your name]'.
8. If you don't hear anything over the radio for a while, there's probably something wrong with it. Check that your earpiece is in correctly and that you're on the right channel.
9. To start up your radio in the morning and let everyone know you're on comms, attach your earpiece and say 'radio check'. Repeat this whenever you make a change to your radio. The response to 'radio check' is 'good check'.
10. If you can, go for the over-ear D-ring connection, rather than the in-ear 'covert' connection. I found it made my ear very itchy. Sometimes people invest in their own earpieces, for comfort.
11. Radios, funnily enough, emit radiation, so try not to put them near your kidneys or your ovaries. Try to wear the radio, therefore, on your hip.

Table 3.2 Rate card

POSITION	DAILY RATE	WEEKLY RATE
Runner	£130–£155	£500–£550
Junior Researcher	£150–£180	£550–£825
Researcher	£150–£200	£600–£930
Assistant Producer	£250–£300	£800–£1,100
Producer	£400–£500	£1,150–£1,450
Director	£700–£1,000	£1,400–£1,700

Rate cards

Nobody likes to talk about money, but we must, as it's vital that you know how to pitch your services appropriately and avoid underselling yourself. PMs (or whoever recruits you) will ask you for your rate. Pitch too high, and you come across as arrogant or unrealistic; pitch too low, and you come across as cheap. At every stage in your television career, you should establish your daily and weekly rates, gradually increasing them as you become more experienced. You should increase your rate slightly with every job you do, as this reflects your increased worth as someone who has gained more experience. As a runner, you can increase your daily rate by £10 with every job; with all other positions in television, you should increase your weekly rate by £50–£100 per job. Always ask for £50–£100 more than you would be happy with, then let the PM negotiate you down. The best-case scenario is they pay you more; the worst-case scenario is they pay you what you're happy with. As a runner, you may be asked to invoice for your time if it's a short job, or you will be paid by PAYE if it's a longer gig. Researchers and APs are paid on the payroll (PAYE); producers and directors are expected to invoice. If you invoice, you are responsible for paying tax on your earnings: you should register for tax self-assessment on the UK Government website. It seems daunting but is actually very easy to do.

The rate card shown in Table 3.2 is a guideline that is true at time of writing, but the given rates will change depending on inflation etc. For a fully up-to-date rate card, please check the BECTU website. BECTU is the union for TV and film cast and crew; they offer support, mentoring schemes and expense allowances for members.

Summary

- Be proactive and positive
- Network with others on the production team
- Make sure you have the right kit

Chapter 4

Researcher

There are several different ways to step up from runner to researcher. All of them, however, involve speaking to a production manager (PM).

The easiest route is if you're an office runner. In an office, it will be widely accepted that the next step up from your current role will be as a researcher. as the office runner, you'll also have inside knowledge about which productions are crewing up, so you will be best placed to speak to the PM on whichever project you're interested in and ask for a researcher role on it. Make your keenness and preference known as early as possible; make sure you're very good at the job you're already doing (so that your competence is proven); and make sure that you're friendly with everyone – all these will serve you well for that step up.

If you are working as a production runner on long productions or studio shoots, then you may have less insight into when the next jobs are coming up, but your first port of call is still the PM. Start by doing an excellent job as a production runner – then approach the PM and raise your interest in becoming a researcher. For example, if you are working on a repeatable series, tell them how much you have enjoyed your time on this production and ask if you can be involved in the next series as a researcher. If it is not a repeatable series, tell them you are interested in stepping up to a researcher role and ask if they have any other productions coming up for which they need a researcher. Follow up on the conversation with an email reminding them of your interest and your CV.

It's a similar situation if you're a studio runner, although you're less likely to have as much contact with the PM as studio jobs will typically be much shorter. If the PM is not on set at any point, you should be able to get their contact details from the call sheet. You may, of course, already have them, if the PM is the person who employed you (although if you're employed directly by the studio, this may not be the case). If you're working on a comedy, talent or reality show, it will certainly help to have a personal interest or background in the topic of the show – that way you can offer something extra to the PM. For example, if you're working on a comedy series and you

DOI: 10.4324/9781003294009-5

used to write or perform sketches, bring that up in conversation as a way to support your interest in becoming a researcher.

If you are an *ad hoc* runner, working on a variety of shows, then you'll need to cultivate relationships with as many PMs as possible and pursue multiple avenues until they yield a researcher job. Alternatively, if you are running for several different jobs but know which genre you want to work in, try to focus your work in that area and capitalise on your interest in your job applications and emails. At this stage, your greatest assets are charm, enthusiasm, and competence. If at any point you are struggling to get the contacts to step up, or even to find out about upcoming researcher jobs you can apply for, ask if there is a Facebook group you can join. There are several groups that are still the default advertising platforms for TV jobs – but there tend to be separate groups for runners versus other editorial jobs. Make sure you join the right group. At this stage in your career, it's not worth signing up for a talent site like Talent Manager or Talent Bases – you'll want to do that as soon as you get your first researcher job.

You may start off as a junior researcher – but even if this is your job title, you will likely be doing the same job as a researcher. If you have a degree in science or history, and are capitalising on this to work on a specialist factual documentary series, then you will need less time to familiarise yourself with the subject matter than someone coming to the programme from a purely TV-oriented background. You will also have plenty of transferable skills from your degree, such as identifying reliable sources, finding at least two citations for any fact and arranging information into a structure that makes narrative sense. However, someone from a TV background will have other skills – more of a sense of what makes a good story for television, for example, or an idea of how to manage talent and identify attention-grabbing hooks. Whatever your background, you simply need to use your relevant experience to your advantage in a researcher role – and learn fast to catch up with the other skills that you need to acquire. The rest of this chapter will prime you on those very skills.

Be the best researcher

Congratulations on your first researcher job! Now, what exactly are you supposed to do?

The first thing to establish is to whom you are reporting. Are you working with a single director? Are you supporting several directors across a series? Are you supporting a pool of assistant producers (APs)? Once you have established your hierarchy, then it helps to determine exactly how your nominal bosses like to work. This is usually an unwritten, nuanced relationship that takes strong people skills and sensitivity to set up. A director may be initially surprised, but ultimately grateful, if you ask outright how they would like the information presented to them (in a research document, in a series of emails, in a table etc.). Whether you establish this through a frank conversation or through a gentle back-and-forth, it is the most important aspect of your future working relationship.

The information that you're looking for will vary depending on which stage the production is at. This chapter will take you through all the different stages of a production, and the researcher's role in each of them.

Base-level research

In this scenario, the programme or series has been commissioned and you are brought on at the beginning of the project. If it has not already been supplied, ask for the treatment so that you can familiarise yourself with the idea that has been pitched to and commissioned by the channel. The story will usually evolve significantly over the course of the production, but the treatment document will give you a detailed baseline from which to start.

The next step is to discuss with the director their vision for the storyline and if there are any specific research points they want you to pursue. If this is still open to development, or if your director hasn't started on the project yet, you should familiarise yourself as much as possible with the subject matter to flesh out the information supplied in the treatment.

You will need to gain a thorough understanding of the full context and background information and be confident enough in your knowledge to explain it to the director (who will then structure this research into their script). However, you should be doing more than amassing facts. There must be purpose to your research: always keep the overall story in mind when you're researching and think about how that information fits with the theme of the series or programme. Think about how you might effectively tell the story around these facts – where you might go to film, for example, or what single objects might unlock a broader history around which the director could construct a sequence, what facts the audience might be surprised to learn.

For example, if you are researching a programme about animals and you discover that an ant can carry fifty times its own bodyweight, that's a great fact on its own – but what will take this information to the next level, and earn you a brilliant reputation as a researcher, is if you find out exactly what that weight is equivalent to and provide examples. So: an ant can carry fifty times its own bodyweight, the equivalent of two mushrooms. Now the audience has a clear image in their heads of a tiny ant carrying two big mushrooms, and it brings that piece of information to life in a very visual way.

Case study: Roman Empire

My very first Researcher job was on a series about the Roman Empire. I had just graduated with a Classics degree, so I already had a strong understanding of the subject matter – but what I didn't understand was how to turn that subject matter into a compelling story for television. I supplied my director with pages and pages of factoids, artefacts and historical summaries – but he would look through them and ask for something different, or tell me that they wouldn't help him structure his story. I was crestfallen. I thought I had supplied him with fascinating research. Then he put it in simple terms: more sex, death and murder.

What he meant by this was stories that would grab the audience's attention. Stories that would make them want to keep watching the programme to find out more. Stories that would keep them on the edge of their seat and almost shock them into learning more about the Romans.

With this in mind, I found him the spiciest stories I could (which were also grounded in historical fact). The next step was to find out how best to tell them through locations that our presenter, Mary Beard, could visit, or objects she could handle, so that the audience could experience the story visually, as well as aurally. It is TV's distinct advantage over radio: being able to take people to places they might not have the time or money to visit for themselves. To show them objects that might otherwise be inaccessible, such as the storerooms of museums or closed-off sites, or to frame the information around a single statue in a way that brings the cold marble to life. This is the researcher's job: to find the information that will allow the director to unleash the full power of television as an audiovisual storytelling medium.

Current affairs research

The case study above looked at a story that was based in the past, where the events of the production had already happened and the sources were well established. For current affairs stories, however, you don't have that luxury. Often there are time constraints on the structure of the story, such as specific events you need to film, or difficulty accessing the correct information. In this situation, you have to be good at performing under pressure, and you have to identify a reliable source on the ground. Usually, this is a fixer, but it might be a scientist, academic or other local expert on the story in question. You'll need to use your people skills to build a strong relationship with that person, and while email is a viable way of doing this, it is infinitely preferable to develop that relationship over the phone. You'll also get answers more quickly that way.

Use your contact wisely. Don't rely on them for all your information – make sure you do your own research as well, and use them to supply the details you can't find through other sources. With a fast-turnaround, event-specific, high-pressure project, you will also need to quiz them on the practicalities of access and filming – issues you would normally think about as an AP. (For more on this, take a look at the next chapter.) Mentally walk through the shoot in your head and note down everything that could possibly go wrong and all the things you would need to know in order to execute that shoot – you can run this past your director to make sure you haven't missed anything. They will appreciate your initiative.

If you are producing current affairs, it is particularly important that you have accurate facts at your fingertips. Make sure you have all the up-to-date information, and that you can get hold of your contact quickly if you need to check something with them that is time-sensitive.

In-production research

You've done the baseline research, your director or producer has written the beat sheets (which are like a roadmap for the script, a brief outline of the key points in the storyline), and everyone has a rough idea of where they're going with the story.

As the production ramps up and the story evolves into a script, your work becomes less immersive and more responsive. If you have been creating beautifully formatted research documents, now is the time to start supplying most of your research in email format. Make sure you keep track of all the information you send via email though, as you may need it again when you get to the fact-checking stage.

Production is one of the most exciting stages to be a researcher, as you will be actively shaping the scripts with the information you supply. However, it can also be a high-pressure time when there's a risk that your accuracy might slip. In the mission to create an effective balance between the hard facts and a compelling story, directors will turn to you to approve their phrasing of certain key events or points in the story. You will have to be very clear on what is accurate and what pushes the boundaries of factual integrity. For example, if a historical fact is debated, you can advise that it be phrased or introduced as 'some sources say' or 'it is said that' or 'some believe that'. This way you are introducing the idea of debate, while allowing the scriptwriter to continue their story arc without having to pause and explain a complex theoretical academic debate. When you are advising the directors on how to craft these compromises, make sure you do not also compromise your own integrity as a researcher. Even if it means having a difficult conversation with the director, it will be worth it in the end – you will earn more respect as a researcher, the commissioner will be happy with the integrity of the programme, and you will have a clear conscience in terms of the information being supplied to the viewing audience.

A cautionary note on this last point – it is sometimes difficult to know when to stop pushing with a difficult conversation. If the dispute is escalated to the executive on the project, and they make a final decision, then you should stop pushing, even if you think their decision is wrong. As long as you have made your concerns clear, then your integrity is assured. The television industry has a reputation for sensitive egos – this, unfortunately, is true in many cases. Sometimes, the battle is not worth the fight.

Fact checking

Some broadcasters require a fact-checked script to be supplied as part of the programme deliverables. If you have not been across all your sources during the production process, this can be time-consuming and frustrating. As a rule, it is only the commentary (voiceover) that you will be fact checking; any contributors should take responsibility for the accuracy of their own interview content.

It is good practice to have at least two reliable sources for each fact. Wikipedia does not count as a reliable source. General or obvious statements, such as 'England, a tiny nation in northern Europe', do not need sources. However, any specific statements such as 'Henry was a Tudor king', and 'for over a thousand years, this island was uninhabited' do require fact checks.

These fact checks will usually take place as the film is reaching picture-lock, but before the voiceover (VO) is recorded, so that any inaccuracies can be changed before the VO is added. If you do notice a factual inaccuracy, raise it as quickly as possible with your director or series producer (SP), and suggest a solution to the problem. This is particularly important if the mistake is contained within the visual assets, which will need to be re-edited.

Essential skills: phone manner

Picking up the phone can be daunting, especially if you're just starting out and need to build your confidence on your subject matter. When I was starting out, my two biggest fears were that I would not introduce myself properly, and that I would forget to say something important during the phone conversation. Within the first few sentences, you need to introduce yourself, explain why you are calling and where you're calling from. Sometimes you will have to ask someone a strange or very specific request, which can take some explaining. Below is a foolproof formula for that introduction, which you can adapt as necessary.

Hello, my name is [name], I'm calling from [production company], we're looking for a [contributor/location/prop] for a new [programme/series] we are making about [general topic] for [broadcaster]. I was wondering if you might be able to help me?

In order to remember everything I needed to mention in that phone conversation, I used to prepare myself a Post-it note containing the following details:

• The person's name. If you don't know their name, make a note of the name of the person who picks up the phone, and make sure to repeat their name at the end of the call – e.g. 'thank you so much, Brenda. I appreciate your help with this!' It helps to build a personal connection.
• Their phone number (so you can dial again without looking it up if they don't answer the first time)
• An alternative phone number – e.g. mobile/cell number (in case you don't get through to the first number you tried)
• Main question
• Additional details needed – e.g. date/time/email address

After enough Post-it note phone calls, this checklist will start to become a mental one, and the calls will feel a lot more natural. It also helps to imagine that the person you are calling could be your new best friend by the end of the phone call. Make sure your phone voice is your friendliest voice – if you are naturally gifted with a sense of humour, then this is an enormous advantage.

As a general rule, phone calls are preferable to emails – you can start with an introductory phone call, for example, and then follow up with an email. That email is much more likely to be answered, because you have already built up a relationship over the phone. There are a few situations, however, where you absolutely must pick up the phone as opposed to emailing:

• If you need a quick answer (like a filming location for the following day)
• If you need to brief a contributor before an interview (you'll find out more about this in the chapter on producing, but you should never send them their question list via email. Always ask to discuss their interview topics with them on the phone).
• If someone is being difficult in emails (sometimes that's just their writing style; difficult people are almost always nicer over the phone)
• If someone has raised a sticky problem (such as a difficulty with transport bookings)
• If someone threatens to pull out of the production (I have never known this situation to be resolved via email. Over the phone, however, the contributor is brought back on board nine times out of ten).

Golden rules

Golden Rule 1: It's OK to say 'I don't know'

Whatever you are researching, you must strive to be thorough in your work, accurate in what you write and say, and confident in your knowledge. At the same time, you can't possibly know everything about a topic, especially if it's new to you, so don't be afraid to say 'I don't know' – just always follow it up with 'I'll check and get back to you'.

Golden Rule 2: Do NOT copy-paste information!

Readers can always tell when information has been directly lifted. You should be adding value to the information – the director can look up a wiki page themselves – your job is to place that information in context with supplementary research, check its accuracy, and present it in a format that the director can easily use to inform and structure their script.

For example, a director may ask how many wind farms are owned by a certain energy company in the US. Your search will find detailed information on the megawattage of the wind farms, their addresses, the number of turbines and the output capacity. To a director, this is just a series of numbers. As a researcher, you should process that information into TV-friendly terms. For example, the energy company owns four wind farms in the US: two in California, one in Texas and one in Wyoming. Altogether, these wind farms produce enough energy to power nearly 100,000 homes. The Texas site supplies almost half that energy, despite having the fewest turbines. The director can then easily process that information into a line of VO that might go something like: 'Texas: home to this company's most powerful wind farm'.

Elaine Rhodes has three years' experience as a Researcher, working across a range of specialist factual documentaries, from ancient history to 9/11 and everything in between. She has a strong reputation in the TV industry for her dedicated attitude to research.

Interview with Elaine Rhodes

My route into becoming a specialist factual researcher did not follow the more traditional runner to researcher route. After graduating with a history degree, and working for a number of years in a different sector, I went back to school to get a Master's degree in Public History. I loved learning about the past, and this course seemed to offer the possibility of turning this passion into a job.

Public History is any forum in which historical narratives are crafted for the public, including museums, archives, gallery spaces, video games, literature and, of course, television. It explores not only what historical narratives are chosen and how they are packaged, but how audiences engage and consume the stories that are presented, and how this contributes to public discourse about the past.

As a history student, you're often led to believe that teaching is one of the few viable options after graduation. I knew that there must be a job that somehow combined history and television, but that was as far as my knowledge went. It was a closed world. Thankfully, I had a wonderful tutor, who encouraged me to volunteer with a visiting documentary film crew that were making a show about Guy Fawkes. It was only for a few days, but I used this opportunity to soak as much up as possible, and ask (many, many) questions.

Ahead of the filming day, although I was volunteering as a runner, I asked the producer if there was any research I could help with. There was. Whether you're on work experience, working as a runner or starting out in your first researcher role, the first port of call is to ask your line manager how you can help. By doing so, I gained research as well as runner experience, I had more context for the content being captured, as well as the satisfaction of seeing how my research informed the interview questions. I learned how being armed with the right information not only helps the producers to access information more efficiently, it facilitates a good working relationship by showing the contributors you have done your homework.

Perhaps the most valuable takeaway was the practical advice shared by the producer, who told me that if I wanted to pursue a career in specialist factual, I should create a Talent Manager Profile. It's like LinkedIn, but for TV. It sounds small, but you don't know what you don't know. By sharing this information, she opened the door to the closed world. So, I made a profile and two weeks later I had an interview. A week after that I was in my first researcher role on an established ancient history series, and the rest was history (the terrible pun intended...).

The responsibilities of a researcher are multiple and varied, and can be roughly divided into two blocks, pre-production and post-production (aka before filming, and after filming). Pre-production responsibilities included producing tailored research notes for the APs, researching archival material and the permissions needed for certain on-screen images, and helping support the general organisation of the shoot. The series' episodes ranged from Ancient Rome and Iron Age Sweden to Ancient Egypt. One day I was producing notes on the popularity of fish sauce in the Roman Mediterranean, the next I was delving into Ancient Egyptian beliefs about the afterlife.

It's important for research notes to be comprehensive but concise. It's also good practice to make sure you add footnotes containing page numbers. This is so that should a colleague need to follow up a particular point, they can easily locate the original information and relevant page. Producers might not have time to read a twenty-page article about the garum trade in Roman Africa. However, they are more likely to be able to absorb a summary page covering the article's key takeaways (e.g. this condiment was the 'ketchup' of the ancient world). So that information was as accessible as possible, each time I delivered a set of notes, I also made sure to email the notes alongside any article pdfs.

Because the information you deliver to your team helps to shape the story being told, it's essential to know what the deadlines are. The shooting schedule informs when each shooting script should be ready by, and so if you are familiar with these touchpoints, you will know when the key facts need to be locked in. Being organised also helps you to anticipate what your producers might need next. If no notes were urgently needed, I would use the time to read up around any upcoming topics. As a researcher, you're not expected to know everything about everything, but you should always do your best to find out as much as you can. If you have time, it's handy to become familiar with upcoming material so that you know which resources to consult when you need to. For example, is there is a particularly instrumental book on the topic that you should get your hands on?

On the other hand, I found that reactivity is equally important. A production is an ever-evolving beast, and this means what is required of the researcher is also subject to change. One day you might be trying to find the most bawdy ancient Roman graffiti, the next you are urgently trying to work out how to order a haunch of pig from a remote Swedish island to be used in an experiment designed to demonstrate the efficacy of Viking armour. It is all a learning curve, but as long as you get stuck in, are transparent about your workload and communicative with your colleagues when it comes to priorities, you should not go too far wrong.

As with any role, there are challenges. When I first started as a researcher, I found the biggest learning curve came during the post-production stage. This is when filming is completed and fact checking kicks into high gear. As the researcher, part of my job was to look through the scripts the way a teacher does when marking homework, critical eye and red pen at the ready. Specialist factual content should be engaging and exciting, but crucially, it has to be accurate. If the script isn't accurate, it's a work of fiction masquerading as fact, which is misleading and unfair to the audience. Sometimes a sentence might sound good, but not be completely accurate. For example, a line might read 'Tutankhamun was the greatest pharaoh that ever lived'. Although he is arguably the most well known, many scholars would posit that his reign was not as impressive as some of his pharaonic peers. If possible, it's helpful to offer an alternative. E.g. 'Tutankhamun was a key part of the famous/majestic 18th dynasty'.

In the beginning, as the most junior team member, I sometimes found it slightly nerve-wracking to say when things were inaccurate or needed changing, especially if it was a story element my colleagues were particularly excited about. Fact checking can be time-pressured, and so sometimes things inevitably fall through the cracks. During one particularly fast-paced history series, the time allocated to fact checking was tight. On top of this, we received compliance notes from our legal team that needed to be actioned ASAP. Picture-lock was imminent and I had noticed some factual errors that needed to be addressed. Ideally, scripts should be locked and fact-checked well ahead of picture-lock, preferably at fine-cut stage. I had been nervous to flag that some facts would need amending so late in the day. On top of this, it was clear there was insufficient time to give the compliance notes the attention they required. The volume of work felt overwhelming, and so I decided to communicate this to my managers, who responded by adjusting the deadlines. I learned that ultimately, the content has to be accurate and legally compliant. As my manager told me at the time, it was my job to give them the facts and flag any issues so that they can make decisions with all of the information laid out in front of them.

Finding the required information can be time-consuming and frustrating. Not all evidence is low-hanging fruit. But it's incredibly satisfying to finally find the thing you've been searching for, or stumble upon something new or surprising that will help propel the story forward. Research is investigation. Getting to put on a detective cap and track down the facts is one of the best things about the job. You never know what you're going to find.

Development Researcher

In a production company, the Development department is responsible for coming up with, then 'developing' or working up, then pitching, ideas for TV shows. Many researchers make their step up through development – junior development researcher roles are regularly advertised and usually require little to no prior experience. Working in development gives you great training in what makes a good TV idea, both from the creative side and from the practical (or political) side of fulfilling the demands of a commissioner.

Being a development researcher involves patience and creativity, as well as a lot of resilience. This section will outline how to be an effective development researcher, including tips on how to write up good pitches and treatments.

The idea

Coming up with, or identifying, a good idea for a TV show is very hard work. And a lot of what makes an idea successful is to do with the timing, the commissioner and the target audience.

Sometimes commissioners will put out tenders, so production companies have an idea of what topics they're looking for. These will come through to the development executive, who will then allocate the development of these ideas to members of their team.

Most of the time, however, you are just trying to find a good idea that the commissioners will like. Usually, production companies will specialise in a certain genre of TV, so that will guide your search for ideas – for example, if the company specialises in history programmes, you should be looking for new historical and archaeological discoveries; if the company specialises in travel, you should be thinking about new formats or anticipating the next popular destination.

The companies will also have their favoured commissioners, which will inform the types of ideas you're looking for and the way you write them up. You're writing to two audiences at this stage: the commissioner, who will have their own programme preferences, and the channel's audience, who will be a certain demographic.

These demographics often have characters that help inform your writing and pitching style. For example, ITV's audience is termed Auntie Beryl, a woman of a certain age who is generous and kind but enjoys a certain amount of people-watching, hand-wringing and *Schadenfreude*. Channel 5's audience, by contrast, is characterised as the 'chatty cabbie', a well-meaning working-class gent who wants to watch programmes that will allow him to impress his customers with new interesting facts.

When you're looking for ideas, make sure you have a clear idea of which ideas will resonate best with which audience, so that your executives know where to pitch these ideas.

As a general rule, when you're searching for ideas, you should be looking either for new information or a new perspective on a popular concept. This also applies to generating format or reality shows – particularly in this instance, you should be brainstorming new approaches to well-known format models. These are usually easier to get past a commissioner than a brand-new concept – although if those new concepts are appropriately researched and developed, they can be the real money-spinners for a production company.

The pitch

You've identified a good idea. You've run it past the development exec and they think it's got potential. Now you need to write the pitch.

There are three different types of pitches: the elevator pitch, the paragraph pitch and the one-pager.

The elevator pitch is one, maximum two sentences that describe what your idea is and why it's new and exciting. This can then be expanded to a full paragraph, which should go into more detail about how the idea would work and why it is different from anything else. The one-pager would be something you might submit to a commissioner at the early stages of the idea development. It should have a punchy, attention-grabbing opening line, then the rest of the document should walk the commissioner through your vision for the programme or series, suggesting filming locations, interviewees or, for a reality/format show, filming logistics and format rules.

Writing a pitch is an excellent exercise in learning what exactly is important and relevant for a television audience. You might be fascinated by a particular scientific discovery but if you are not able to make it interesting and relevant to your commissioner and their audience, you will not get the pitch past elevator stage and you will not be a very effective development researcher. The good news is, a kind executive will help you to learn this technique, or you'll learn it by trial and error.

As you develop your eye and ear for strong TV ideas, and as you develop your writing skills to help you hone those powerful pitches, here are a few tips to get you started:

How would you tell the story verbally? I certainly find it easier to tell someone about something interesting than to write about it. If you're struggling to find the right words, maybe go for a walk or sit in a café and dictate your verbal explanation into your phone. Then when you return to the office you can listen back to it, and it might help your write-up.

Once you've finished a pitch, print it out and reread it before you send it off to be checked. Are there any typos? Does it make sense? Have you explained the idea well enough?

Plan out the film as though it were your project, as though you were producing the film. Visualise how the story will pan out in the finished programme – and then write it up.

If someone else on your team has reviewed and rewritten your work, study what changes they have made. How can you learn from what they have changed in your document? Is there a different way of formatting the information that they prefer? How have they rearranged your paragraphs to make it punchier? And most importantly, how can you apply that to your next document?

Finally, don't be downhearted if several ideas in a row don't get past the elevator pitch stage. It might not be the right time for those ideas, or it might be that something very similar has been commissioned too recently. Even if you were very invested in those ideas, don't take the rejection personally. Television development is a constant cycle of creativity, research, revision, rejection. The ideas are put through the commissioning distillery until they emerge more refined and more powerful. Ultimately, it's a positive process, even if it doesn't feel like it at the time! If you do ever get downhearted, remember – the *Great British Bake Off* took ten years to develop. Ten years.

The treatment

The pitch is so strong that you've been asked to write up a one-pager, and that one-pager has caught the attention of a commissioner. Now it's time to develop it further into a treatment.

Some companies create treatments as written documents, others prefer to format them as decks (see next section). The purpose of the treatment is to walk the commissioner through the show, step by step.

You should expect your treatment to be between four and ten pages if it's a Word document, and 10-20 slides if it's a deck. In both cases, it should be extremely visual – remember that this is the unique selling point (USP) of TV, that we can show people as well as tell them stories. Make sure you have plenty of photos in your treatment, to give the commissioner a flavour of what they might see in the finished programme. Your treatment should start by outlining the hook (why this, why now), then the overall concept (what the story is) and finally, the programme outline (or if it's a series, a summary of each episode). Remember that you are not just trying to persuade a commissioner to buy the series, you are also creating a blueprint for the production team that will eventually take on the show when it gets commissioned. With each episode outline, you should be thinking through the logistics of filming and the practical aspects to storytelling.

Case study: history of maths

When I was a Development Researcher, I worked up a four-part documentary about the history of maths (which, incidentally, got commissioned). It was particularly challenging to come up with creative ways to explain some key mathematical concepts – after all, history lends itself to storytelling, but maths is so much more theoretical! For the earlier episodes, the planning was fairly straightforward, such as using the Parthenon in Ancient Greece to explain Pythagorean triangles and the Golden Ratio, or employing the timelessly beautiful setting of Venice to explain the invention of the decimal point, or explaining the Fibonacci sequence through its manifestation in nature. But when we got to theories about infinity and quantum mechanics, I was rather stuck. The development executive worked with me to come up with innovative ways of explaining them, using abstract settings, animation and lab-based experiments to show the theories, rather than just trying to explain them in words.

Again, we come back to the most important thing to bear in mind when you're making television: it's visual as well as audio. It sounds so simple, but it's very easy to get tied up in complex factual information and forget what medium you are actually researching for. It is just as important to show as it is to tell. In a way, this takes the pressure off you as a researcher – you don't have to explain everything with facts and figures; you can apply your creativity to convey the story in a more effective and memorable way. This is also what makes you stand out from academics – they only operate in words, whereas you have so much more to play with.

The deck

Some commissioners, particularly in the US, prefer to view their treatments as decks rather than written documents. These should still follow the basic principles of what constitutes a treatment, but will present the information in a more visual way, with less information on each page. Below are my top ten treatment tips for writing decks:

MAKE IT VISUAL. Use the title page to say as much as you can about the show with a picture. They say an image speaks a thousand words, and they're right! Identify your three key selling points of the show and put them together in a bold statement image, along with the title of the show. Even better if you can use Photoshop and create a really cool composite picture.

KEEP IT CONSISTENT. Find a background design that subtly creates a mood for the show. But don't make it too elaborate – you've got to be able to read what the page says too. Your company may already have an accepted format for how they like to present decks – if you want to change that format to reflect the idea of the show, make sure you check with your exec first.

TARGET AUDIENCE. If you're writing for a specific channel, keep its typical target audience, its colour scheme and its logo in mind. Make it easy for the channel to see that programme idea in their schedule; show them clearly how it fits into their existing broadcasting.

MIND READ. Put yourself in the position of the commissioner. They get several treatments every day; they'll probably read it in an Uber on their way to a meeting while also worrying about their 5-year-old with chicken pox, so if they can't get past the first two pages, they won't read on. Make sure they understand what the show is about within the first two pages, and are intrigued enough to want to continue.

CHECK YOUR TEXT. If you wrote two sentences, can you say it in one? If you wrote ten words, can you explain it in five? Like an advertising copywriter, you want to communicate as much information as possible in as few words as possible. Get creative with this, try out different ways of expressing things until you land on the best form of words.

USE YOUR IMAGINATION. Let it run away with you! Draw out a full episode, think about how it would work, invent characters, create tension. By doing this, you not only visualise it for the commissioner, but you also anticipate potential production problems. Many a treatment has almost been completed, but then when the sample episode is written out, the fatal flaw is discovered...and you have to start again from scratch.

DAFONT.COM. You're a creative. A PowerPoint template and Times New Roman are not going to impress. Download a new font from dafont.com that is in the style of the show – but check how it converts to pdf before sending it off. If it doesn't convert correctly, it may end up looking more like a beauty pageant show than the next *Jackass*...which could lose you that commission.

LOTS OF PICTURES. Television is a visual medium. Yes, I keep saying it, and yes, it's obvious, but if your experience is in an academic or copywriting setting, then you may be more familiar with words than visuals. Anything you say comes with a strong mental image, so make sure you and the commissioner have the same image by backing it up with a real one.

EASY TO READ. Choose a font colour that stands out from the background you've chosen, make the text big enough and space it out nicely so that your text isn't too intimidating. A background in graphic design or a strong eye for visual layouts is very useful when designing treatment decks.

TIME TO PLAY. Play around with all the formatting options available to you. Sometimes just adding a shadow here, a glow effect there or a subtle background colour tint will turn your dull treatment into something stunning. You should take a lot of time over your treatments and make sure you're completely happy with them before sending them off.

The sizzle

The commissioner likes the treatment, but before they part with their channel's money, they would like to see an example of how the show might work. This is where the sizzle comes in.

This will be a short film (maximum two minutes long) that's like a trailer for the show you're planning to make. Of course, you won't have shot any material yet, so you will have to construct your sizzle out of stock footage or archive from previous shows.

The first step to creating a sizzle is to write the script. Write it in the style of a trailer, so short, punchy sentences, such as:

> One man. Twelve women. Four weeks to find The One. Welcome to *The Bachelor*.

> Or

> 1200 BC. A civilisation vanishes without a trace. A historian, an archaeologist and a former FBI detective team up to uncover what happened in: *Time Scene Investigators*.

Next, you'll need to find visuals to go with that VO. Your production company may already have a bank of archive footage, or you may have to buy in stock footage from companies such as Getty or Pond5. Check the procedure with your exec, and then format your audio and visual elements in a table like the one shown in Table 4.1.

This is the basic layout of a script – you'll come back to it in the sections on Producing and Directing. Making sizzles is a great way to familiarise yourself with a process that will become your bread and butter in your future TV career.

Once you've identified the clips you want (plus a few spare), you will need to send them to your technical team to get them ingested into the edit. Unless you can edit yourself, you will then be paired with an editor, who will assemble the clips according to your script. The idea will evolve as you see it take shape – you may have to rewrite the script, for example, or

Table 4.1

VISUAL	AUDIO
Pond5 clip 153423 YouTube clip 'child in care home 1'	Five children who need a loving home
Getty clip 698421 Pond5 clip 'family in home' YouTube clip 'empty crib'	Five parents looking to adopt
Graphic text on top of YouTube clip 'families in front of houses'	Instant Family: inside the UK's adoption system

source different visuals at short notice. You should also have in mind which music you want behind your sizzle – this, too, should communicate something about the style of the show. Your editor will be very familiar with TV music libraries; they will be able to advise on music choices and then cut the visuals to the music.

Make sure you show the film to your exec when you're happy with it – but leave plenty of time to action their changes. Don't take their changes personally – remember, they have many more years of experience in this industry and they know what works. Take their notes graciously and act on them, or if they don't work, consult the exec and explain the problem. Suggest an alternative solution – or if you are stuck, brainstorm with them to figure out how to make the sizzle sparkle.

The commission

Congratulations, your idea has been commissioned! You may be asked to do a little further development to bring it up to production stage. You may be offered to work as the researcher on the commissioned programme – or you could ask to adopt that role if the offer is not forthcoming. It is fairly common for this step to happen, as you will be best placed to work on the production, having already done the initial research and built up relationships with potential contributors. A word of warning here: don't be worried or offended if the production team have their own vision for where to take the programme, but be clear on anything that was sold with it, such as the participation of a particular presenter.

If your idea is commissioned, make sure to add this at the very top of your CV. It tells your future employers that you are able to recognise a good idea, research it thoroughly, and write it up in a way that is attractive to a commissioner and a TV audience. It is a very valuable string to your bow.

Another option at researcher stage is in archive. Searching for archive takes great patience, an eye for detail, out-of-the-box thinking and excellent negotiating skills. It's not everyone's cup of tea, but if it's yours, it can lead to a very lucrative career. Archive producer Emily Mayson describes how she started out her TV career as an archive researcher.

Archive researcher: interview with Emily Mayson

When I started out in TV, I didn't know archive producing was a job. Now, people think that I work in a library. I clarify by saying I look after the archive footage and photographs in documentaries.

While still at school, I gained work experience in post-production houses and on set every chance I could. I wanted to be a movie director. My TV contacts advised me not to do a film degree (much to the relief of my parents), so I studied linguistics. However, I spent most of my time running the Drama Society and stage-managing theatre shows.

During and after university, I had various production assistant roles on feature films and comedy programmes, both on set during filming and in post-production. I also production-managed and produced professionally funded short films, which gave me a good grounding in organising logistics and managing budgets. I was 26 when I decided film wasn't for me and I wanted to move across into Factual TV.

All my contacts were in film and comedy, so I started from scratch, applying for junior roles in factual. I was hired by a small but well-known production company specialising in history documentaries. I don't even have a History GCSE! I was the only permanent member of staff, in an office manager, receptionist and general assistant role. My boss recognised the value in all my previous experience, even though it wasn't in Factual TV. He gave me different roles on various projects alongside my office work – as a production coordinator or researcher.

One project had an archive producer two days a week. His job fascinated me, as I hadn't come across it before. There was a lot of archive needed in that series, so I helped him. He taught me the basics of archive research and producing. I started by looking after newspapers. I spent days at the British Library reading three years' worth of the *News of the World*, looking for a headline an interviewee had mentioned but couldn't remember the year of. I was elated when I found it – and then that interview got cut out!

After that, I helped with other projects that needed some archive, but not enough to warrant an archive producer. I reported directly to the PM and SP. I based my system and spreadsheet on what the archive producer had taught me and gradually tweaked it to make sense for me, including how I managed the commercial side of archive. My boss said it was unusual to find someone whose brain was both logical and creative, and that's what you need for archive – so he kept giving me archive researcher roles on bigger and bigger projects.

When my boss retired and closed the company, everyone knew me as an archive researcher. I went straight into a new job with my old SP. I stayed at that company for multiple projects as an archive researcher. Again, I worked alone and reported to the PM and SP, learning more on every project.

I hope I don't jinx anything by saying that I haven't been out of work since! Companies keep me on back-to-back projects. People with archive experience are always in demand. I know archive producers who work at multiple companies – a day here, a day there – and they always seem to be booked up months in advance. It's a specialist role, but still very diverse, so it's a fun, interesting way to be involved in a production.

The main responsibility for an archive researcher is finding the additional visuals needed to illustrate the programme. Anything that's not specially shot footage (interviews and location filming) or specially created graphics is archive. It needs to be researched, cleared for use, downloaded, logged, labelled and sent over to the edit. This is the job of the archive researcher.

Usually, the edit producer or editor will give you a wish list of what they need. Sometimes you'll work directly from the script or a playout of the work-in-progress cut. As the edit of the programme progresses, the edit team will add to and amend their requests. It's important to stay up to date with what they need and how feasible their requests are.

Often a wish list will have many specific things on it, which you will need to track down. Sometimes it's surprisingly quick and sometimes it takes forever! They will need more general things too. We call it 'wallpaper'. Think about how to fill the screen time if the specific things don't exist or fill little screen time (repeating the same archive is boring). You might need some more abstract shots.

They will ask for impossible things. The sooner you can verify that it doesn't exist, the sooner they can change direction with how they are structuring the narrative. You can make suggestions for what to use instead. You have considerable editorial input as they construct the programme from the archive you find. They might want footage of a particular Ancient Egyptian tomb being discovered in 1799, but film wasn't invented for another 100 years – you'll be lucky to even find an engraving in a newspaper. Instead, give them shots to build an evocative reconstruction sequence of sand, pyramids and close-up digging.

There are a few places to find the archive you need. The first stop is archive libraries – collections of films and images that are set up for licensing for broadcast and publication. They have nearly everything digitised and downloadable on their websites. You will make contacts at these libraries who can help you with research and streamline the licensing process. Building relationships with them increases your value as an archive researcher as you can negotiate better rates.

You might also get archive from contributors who feature in the programme – childhood photos or videos of them doing an academic study, for example. You'll need to get them to sign a release form. This is a legal agreement to license the content for use in the programme.

If neither of these avenues is fruitful, you'll be doing more general research. Sometimes you can find the image you need online. You then contact the website, institution or person who owns the image to introduce yourself and the programme and see if it's possible to use their content. Some places will have their own paperwork; others will need to sign your release form. Don't sign anything yourself as a researcher – give it to your archive producer or PM to check and sign – but do read contracts and flag any potential problems. The more legal documents you read, the less intimidating they are and the more easily you can spot any potential pitfalls. Be sure to ask people up front if they can license for the terms you need and make sure the paperwork is OK. There's nothing worse than finding out you can't license something after the programme is finished and having to replace it at the last minute!

If you can't find the images you need online, you need to reach out to the kinds of places that might be able to help and pick their brains. Do your research. If you need a certain type of Roman artefact, contact Roman museums or archaeologists. If you need a portrait of someone, contact institutions they were involved with. Speak to the researchers and APs – they might have contacts from their factual research who can help.

One of the most frustrating things is when an image is available online but you can't find it from a licensable source. You know it exists, the edit team have fallen in love with it and you have to say they can't have it because it's not clearable. Sometimes you spend days looking for it, only to find it's not the person/place/era you thought it was. The worst situation is when the edit put it in the cut without telling you. They use it as a 'placeholder', but then forget that it's not cleared archive and structure the narrative around it. Invariably, they will label it image1.jpg and you'll spot it weeks later on an EDL (Edit Decision List – a list of all the shots in the cut). They'll say they found it on Pinterest, and you'll spend hours going round in circles online, only to find it's not the right John Smith after all. They'll have to recut the whole story, because their John Smith died before photography was invented. Remember that the first image search engines give you isn't neces- sarily the right person – always check the dates and locations, and follow all the links back to their original source. Often an image will be on multiple sites labelled as the wrong elusive person. You become good at recognising clothing and facial hair from different eras and places that can be a warning sign that something is amiss.

If you've tried everything to clear an image but still haven't been able to track down the owner, talk to your archive producer and PM. There are sometimes ways to use it anyway, if it's good enough resolution – fair dealing/fair use (there are different rules for this in different countries) or await claim (putting money aside in case the copyright holder gets in touch after broadcast) – depending on where the programme is being broadcast. You'll need to consult lawyers and keep a record of everything you've tried to track down the copyright holder to show you've left no stone unturned, so it's always a last resort.

The most exciting part of the job is when you succeed in tracking down the perfect elusive piece of archive. It can take a while with your detective hat on, but it's so exhilarating when you find it!

It's amazing when you come across something that no one has seen for years. You find a listing for something in an obscure library that might be relevant, and then you have a nail-biting wait while the archivist finds it and scans it (typically, they will only be open on Tuesdays and the only person who can work the scanner is on holiday!). And then one day you open an email containing a treasure trove of photographs – of a particular 1930s rum-running ship and its mysterious gangster owner, artists in a Yorkshire fishing village in the 1890s or a top-secret team of WW2 code breakers. I worked on a documentary about the Vietnam War and one of our contributors found a reel of film in his attic labelled 'Vietnam 1967'. He didn't know what it was, so we got it digitised. It had lots of helicopters at his base and a perfect 'Top Gun' shot of him striding towards the camera in his uniform. Another episode was about a Holocaust concentration camp survivor who woke up in a hospital after liberation. We found some old film of the hospital ward and someone in the background seemed familiar. I had the original film re-scanned in 4K resolution and we zoomed in – it was our interviewee. Magical. Finding these gems is such a satisfying part of the job and it makes great telly!

Archive researchers must be very organised. Label and log everything carefully. The log becomes an extension of your memory – it seems like overkill when you first start, but when you've got thousands of pieces of archive in the system, you can't live without it. Back it up regularly! The edit teams also use it to search for the right shots and to see the full descriptions or shot lists. Work closely with the post-production house to make sure everything is in the system in a way that the editors can find what they need easily and be directed to it by the log. It also contains the commercial details of who owns the copyright, any restrictions on use and how much things cost. Teamed with your costing spreadsheet, the log enables you to maintain an overview of costs on each episode and make accurate declarations to archive providers to license everything that appears in the final cut. The log is also helpful at the end of the production when we have to submit the details of all the archive in the programme to the broadcaster. If you put all the useful information in the log and filenames as you go, it saves time later.

The most challenging aspect of the job is managing priorities. It can be very stressful when you are being pulled in multiple directions. When you are working on a series, you've got between three and six edit teams with two episodes each, all editing simultaneously. They all give you urgent requests at the same time. Your brain must constantly switch between different stories and tasks. If you can't find the right archive and send it over to the edits quickly, it can hold them up and impact the schedule. On top of that, you must find time to watch the cuts at various points in the edit and make sure the archive is being used correctly and is on budget – and find suitable cheaper replacements if it's not. There is a lot of pressure, especially if you are the only archive person on a big series.

The kinds of programmes we work on shape our archive research experience and skills. I still primarily work on history programmes – I've become the History round secret weapon in the pub quiz! Many of the first programmes I worked on included a lot of local history. It wasn't the kind of content you would find in an archive library. So very early on I got used to finding local people to help. People are usually excited that a TV company is taking an interest in their area and are eager to help. It's about finding that person with the right connections or the treasure trove of photos. Other fields, like academia, are very similar to villages. Everyone knows each other and you can build a network of people you can ask for advice or archive.

You learn skills on each new project that you take with you to the next one. One day you realise you are a specialist – you know exactly where to look to find obscure archive and you understand quirky parts of copyright law. My early experience in post-production and short films has been a strong foundation to build my archive career on – even though I had no idea that would happen at the time.

Resources

This section details some great websites and locations that are reliable sources for you to start your research, arranged by topic. These are particularly useful for anyone working on specialist factual documentaries.

History resources

Table 4.2 Resources for History programmes

Explorator	https://exploratornews. wordpress.com/	A website that lists all the major archaeological news and discoveries, categorised according to historical period
Livius	www.livius.org/	Great for ancient history. A series of articles about major historical figures, events and locations
LacusCurtius	https://penelope.uchicago.edu/ Thayer/e/roman/home.html	Repository of translations of ancient texts
Queen Victoria's Diary	www.queenvictoriasjournals. org/home.do	There is a wealth of resources about the Victorian era, but a great place to start is always Queen Victoria's Diary, which has been digitised and can be perused online for free
Britannica	www.britannica.com/	A more reliable resource than Wikipedia but just as accessible
Metropolitan Museum of Art	www.metmuseum.org/	Especially useful for identifying objects that can illuminate historical periods. Their articles are reliable sources and well researched
Atlas Obscura	www.atlasobscura.com/	Great for archaeology, science and filming locations
British Library	www.bl.uk/	Membership of the British Library reading rooms is free and opens up a wealth of sources. You have to book a space and order the books in advance.
Erenow	https://erenow.net/	A repository of history books, very useful for consulting sources
Antony Beevor	www.antonybeevor.com/	Always start with Beevor if you're researching WW2

Science resources

Table 4.3 Resources for Science programmes

New Scientist	www.newscientist.com/	Great for easy-to-read updates on the latest scientific discoveries. Try to persuade your production company to subscribe.
Scientific American	www.scientificamerican. com/	More in depth than *New Scientist*. Your production company should subscribe to both.
Cheltenham Science Festival	www.cheltenhamfestivals. com/science-/	A great place to go to spot new presenter talent or snap up the latest popular science books
Nature	www.nature.com/	The gold standard of science journals. Less popular and accessible than *New Scientist*, but the go-to for cutting-edge research

Summary

- Step up through a PM
- Be diligent with your research, but make sure you're trying to understand the storyline too
- Pick up the phone

What to watch

Watch documentaries and think about what research has gone into it. Let's take three examples:

1. Watch a history documentary – say, for example, *Suffragettes* with Lucy Worsley. Listen out for the facts that Lucy tells us about suffragettes. Notice how they are woven into the fabric of the story so you're drawn along with the facts rather than presented with them. Observe which locations Lucy has travelled to in order to 'discover' those facts or that provide an appropriate backdrop for them.
2. Watch a travel documentary, such as Joanna Lumley in Japan. Which areas of Japan does she visit? What does she tell us about those places? What might the researcher have had to find out about

those places that were interesting facts for Joanna to relate? Who does she meet and where does she go to help bring Japan's history and culture to life? These are all things the researcher would have had to find.

3. Watch a natural history documentary, such as David Attenborough's *Blue Planet*. Observe how it's only his voice that carries both the facts and the story. Notice when he's telling us some facts about a beautiful sea creature or remote island, and when he's telling us the story of a male courting a female, or two penguins trying to look after their precious egg in extreme conditions – stories that are relatable and emotional for us audiences. This is how to perfect that fine balance between the facts and the story.

Chapter 5

Assistant Producer

The move from researcher to assistant producer (AP) is probably the hardest to make. This chapter will advise you on how to step up and what to expect once you're an AP. It'll also outline the different paths you can take as an AP to specialise your career path.

Stepping up

If you are an experienced researcher, you will likely already be familiar with many of the responsibilities of an AP, such as speaking to potential contributors, finding and booking locations, and assisting on shoots. However, as an AP, you are expected to take accountability for these tasks while at the same time developing your scripting and storytelling skills, following the example of the directors with whom you'll be working closely.

The only way you will step up from researcher to AP is to ask. And keep asking. If you're a good researcher, you will develop a strong reputation within that role and will be in huge demand from companies, or highly valued if you end up staying with a company for a long time. Your bosses may be reluctant to step you up. If you are looking to advance within the same company, you must express your interest in doing so early, and to everyone who might have the power to help you: producer directors (PDs), production managers (PMs), series producers (SPs), even executive producers (EPs). If you hear of a project that is crewing up, approach the team responsible and express your interest in working on it as an AP.

Every now and then, there are jobs that are specifically advertised as targeted at researcher/AP. These are aimed at either inexperienced APs or experienced researchers ready to step up. Apply for those when they come up and be sure to highlight any existing experience you have of AP-level responsibilities in your cover email. Make sure you ask to be credited as an AP.

If you are not staying at the same company, start applying for AP jobs. You may initially get rejections, but with the right reference or right networking

DOI: 10.4324/9781003294009-6

skills, you may be able to step up straight away. Another tactic is to ask to credit yourself as an AP on your CV – if, for example you were employed as a researcher, but over the course of the project ended up with more AP-level responsibilities. Make sure you check with your SP that they're happy for you to do this, especially if you put them down as your reference for the job. That way you already have an AP credit on your CV, so you won't get rejected as quickly if you start applying for AP jobs.

> The way I stepped up was rather rogue. I was planning to take a couple of weeks off between jobs, when I got an urgent call from a production company asking if I could start work asap on a new project as a researcher. Fortunately, I was in a position where I could afford to turn down the job, so I told them that I was only looking for AP roles. Within an hour, they called me back and offered me an AP position. This was partly a game of chicken and partly a game of building up enough savings to give myself options. I strongly recommend the latter. Money won't buy you happiness, but it does buy you choice.

Now that you're an AP, here's how you go about carrying out your job to the best of your ability and potential.

Be the best AP

Research

Sorry, the research doesn't stop when you stop being a researcher! Especially if you are an AP partnered with a PD, you will be conducting a significant amount of research from scratch. However, at AP level you should be processing the information far more than you might expect a researcher to do. You should be researching with a strong idea of the overall storyline in mind. You and your PD will have a good idea from the treatment (and the PD's vision) about what topics the episode will cover and what the key turning points are in the storyline. You and your PD will jointly tackle a reading list to get a strong idea of the background information. You should discuss with your PD how you would like to pool this information – perhaps in a shared notes document, or separate notes that you send to each other periodically. After you've created a strong knowledge baseline, and from that developed a beat sheet (see p.78), you will get to work on more detailed research on specific story points. Your PD should guide this research according to their evolving script.

If you are overwhelmed with tasks at this stage, you should ask the series researcher (if there is one) to help you with certain research points. It's best to use the researcher's skills for more in-depth requests – for example, specific data points, or a detailed timeline of a complicated series of events. Maximise their attention to detail and keen nose for accuracy, while you focus on the broader overview of information and story thread.

Research example: WW2 netflix series

When I was working as an AP on a series about WW2 for Netflix, my PD and I split the baseline research. I would read books by Antony Beevor, while she developed the storyline. She would regularly request research deep dives to inform specific aspects of the episode and help shape the programme. However, as the production got busier and I was juggling research along with booking contributors and sourcing archive, occasionally I would delegate specific research points to the series researcher. For example, asking for accurate casualty numbers for the Battle of Saipan, or a detailed timeline of Hitler's last moments in his bunker. This allowed the PD to flesh out her script with additional bites of information or build tension within the episode through the commentary lines she was scripting.

Make sure you retain your best practice from your researcher days. Keep track of your research carefully and don't compromise on the reliability of your sources, even if you're under pressure to make a story point work.

Contributors

A significant aspect of your remit is casting contributors. This can be brilliant fun, especially when you land on exciting new talent. The exact qualities you are looking for in a contributor will vary depending on the show you are working on – for example, academics for specialist factual shows versus game show contestants. Our section on the responsibilities of a casting AP will cover the requirements for casting-heavy programmes such as format, game or studio shows. This section will detail what you're looking for in terms of contributors for documentaries.

---

1. **Diversity.** There are plenty of diverse academics and commentators. Do not default to the same male, pale and stale faces. Do your research thoroughly and find some different talent – you may need to look in unexpected places or think outside the box, but make the effort. 'Oh but there aren't any' is not an acceptable answer in this day and age.

2. **New Talent**. Finding new TV talent is one of the best feelings in the world. Programmes often default to the same contributors because they are safe and reliable. New talent may need some coaching, but with a little investment and encouragement, they can take the documentary scene by storm. Having a good relationship with new talent boosts your career, too.

3. **Clarity of Speech**. The contributor must be able to speak clearly without waffling too much. They should be able to summarise information in an effective, punchy way. They should understand the core of the issue or topic and express that in a phrase that briefly captures its significance. They should be able to bring a topic to life with passion and confidence.

4. **Integrity**. They should not only be an expert in their field, but they should also be able to stick to their guns if there is a contentious or debated point, or simply a point on which they would rather not engage. Maintaining this integrity is important and encourages respect.

5. **BONUS: Distinctiveness**. It helps if the contributor has something that makes them stand out. Whether that's a clothing style, a make-up look, a hairstyle, a tattoo or a distinctive way of talking. It should be attention-grabbing without being distracting.

How you find these contributors will, again, depend on the kind of programme you are making. You might look at academic papers, news articles or radio shows. There are some specialised agencies that support academics who want to get into TV. Another useful resource is the Arts and Humanities Research Council, which runs an annual programme supporting PhD students who would like to share their research through the media. A great way to find people who can speak well is to attend events such as the Hay Literary Festival, Cheltenham Literary Festival, Cheltenham Science Festival or the Edinburgh Fringe Festival, on a talent-spotting mission. If you work in development, you may be able to make the case to the production company to support your attendance at one of these festivals.

Once you've identified a shortlist of potential contributors, you should run them past your PD. Whenever you suggest a new contributor, especially if they are a fresh face, you should include their name, a picture, a short bio (which highlights their relevant research/skills) and a clip of them speaking – this should ideally be video, but a podcast could work too. If your PD approves, you should then contact them, asking if they might be interested in appearing on your programme, their availability around the planned filming dates and when they are next available for a chat on the phone or on Zoom. Your email should be brief and to the point: feel free to use this as a template.

> Dear [Prof/Dr if relevant] X, my name is Y, I am contacting you from [production company]. I came across you [briefly outline where this was – TED talk, podcast, festival] and was impressed by [add relevant comment]. I am currently working on a programme/series about Z – would you be interested in appearing on this programme? Our planned filming dates are [insert dates]. What is your availability like during that time? It would be great if we could have a brief chat this week, either on the phone or via Zoom. Let me know when the most convenient time would be to speak.

Before you speak to the contributor, you should have an idea of what function you'd like them to perform in the programme. For example, perhaps their expertise covers certain topics but not all the points you will be covering. Perhaps they can only address one aspect of the programme, albeit a fairly crucial one. Perhaps they are a generalist with knowledge of the whole topic. Make sure you have a clear idea of what you're looking to glean from them – as a general rule, you should not be learning new information at this stage, but rather trying to identify what information they can supply within the storyline you've already established. Sometimes contributors will get a little confused and think that you're trying to get free research from them – in this situation, I find it best to be honest and explain that you have already done the research for the programme; the call is to get an idea of which topics they might be best suited to. Of course, the real reason for the call is to evaluate them as a contributor – but that's a rather too honest approach. I find the suitability line goes down better with sensitive contributors.

When you first start speaking to the contributors, you may find it helpful to have written down a few questions to kick off the conversation. As you get more confident or more familiar with your subject matter, you may not need to prepare questions in advance. You should take detailed notes during the call, or better still, record the call – especially if it's a Zoom. That will allow your director to assess the dynamic with the contributor too – although most of the time, they will trust your judgement.

If, after the conversation, you decide not to film with them, then you should let them down diplomatically. If they were a great potential contributor, but not quite right for the series, then it's helpful to be honest and tell them so. If, however, they were completely unsuitable, either for the series or for television in general, then it is best not to be so honest. Instead, you can cite the series budget as a reason not to use them – for example, that you had only budgeted for a certain number of contributors and had to draw the line somewhere; alternatively, if they live in a place that would be inaccessible for filming, you can cite that as a reason. Another excuse could be the filming schedule, especially if this has undergone a few changes during the process (which it inevitably will!). Your director may also have developed a 'best practice' method for letting contributors down gently – it is worth checking with them before you let someone down. Even if you think that there is absolutely no way you would ever use that contributor again, it is worth maintaining a positive relationship with them – you never know how the situation might develop.

Once you have cast your contributors, you will likely be the primary point of contact with them before, during and after the shoot. You will need to get the following information from them as early as possible:

1. Mobile phone number
2. Email address
3. Availability during the shooting window – plus two weeks either side
4. Location
5. Transport requirements

Before the shoot, you should supply them with the following information:

1. Shoot location
2. Call time (note that this should be approximately an hour after the crew call time – you don't want the contributor hanging around while you're trying to set up)
3. Your phone number, so they can contact you easily if any issues arise on the day
4. Transport information
   a. Parking information if they are driving themselves
   b. Taxi information if they are being collected. The production coordinator (PC) may do this for you.
5. If applicable, a list of topics to be covered in the interview

You, or your director, should prepare a list of interview questions in advance – but it is not best practice to share these questions with the contributor beforehand. You can go through the questions with them on the phone before the interview, but if you send them the written questions, you run the risk that they might either prepare wooden-sounding answers in advance (which ruins the interview) or worse, take issue with the questions themselves and pull out of the production. It is much easier to ask a difficult question in person and discuss it than it is to send a difficult question via email.

You and your director should both attend the interview. It is likely that your director will want to ask the interview questions, although if you want to gain experience, you should ask if you can conduct it. If many interviews are planned, perhaps ask if you can do one of them. Given the fact that you will have cultivated a positive relationship with the contributor, via email and on the phone, you will be their primary point of contact and responsible for ensuring their comfort. On arrival, you should ask if they want any refreshments and point them in the direction of the bathroom.

After the interview, it's worth dropping them a note to thank them for their time and to follow up on any invoicing or payments (which should be conducted via the PM or PC). If you get time, it is a nice touch to write them a thank you card. If they were a good contributor, this helps to maintain a positive relationship going forward – if you work on a lot of similar programmes, you will likely cross paths with that contributor again!

Locations

It's rare to find dedicated location producers or location scouts in Factual TV – unless, of course, you're working on a daytime property show. Even then, due to budget constraints, it may become the responsibility of the AP to find appropriate locations.

As mentioned in the previous section on contributors, exactly what you're looking for in terms of locations will depend on the requirements of the programme. However, there are a few things you should always look out for when you're location scouting:

Indoor locations

1. **Accessibility.** You will need to bring lots of kit into the room(s) in which you're filming. Are there lifts/elevators? Is there a ramp? Can the location provide a trolley? Where is the nearest parking? Can the DoP (Director of Photography) park on site? Perhaps most importantly – is there a coffee shop and/or a sandwich shop nearby, so that you can get refreshments for the crew easily?

2. **Plug sockets.** If you're filming indoors, it is likely the DoP will need a power source for their lights and possibly their camera too.

3. **Soundproofing.** Make sure it's quiet. Is it next to a main road? Can you hear trains? Is it on a flight path? Are the windows double-glazed? Is it near a building site? Is there anything else happening in the venue on that day that might disrupt your interview because of noise? You either need complete silence or a dull consistent rumble of background traffic – but sudden noises will severely disrupt your interview and waste everyone's time. You should spend a bit of time in the location in silence to check, take a video in the room to show the PD and double-check with the location's manager if there is anything happening on your shoot day(s) that might cause additional noise.

4. **Size**. Is the room big enough for you to sit your contributor down, leaving some space behind them, set up lights, put all the DoP's kit in a corner, and have space for you and the director(s) to sit? If you are planning to interview more than one person in the space, how many different setups can you do? How will the background look different for each contributor?

5. **Light**. It is likely that the DoP will want to light the room from scratch, which means that the location will either need to be windowless or have black-out curtains or blinds. Especially in the UK, the weather is very unreliable – you cannot guarantee decent, consistent light.

Outdoor locations

1. **Accessibility**. How easy is it to get there? Where is the nearest parking? How easy is it to transport kit? Where is the nearest accommodation? Where can the crew get food?

2. **Weather**. What are your wet, cold and hot weather contingency plans? Is there a place for people and kit to shelter?

3. **Transport**. If the filming location is a large site, or there are multiple outdoor locations, how will crew and kit be transported between them? Is there rough terrain? Will you need 4x4s?

4. **Permits**. Do you have appropriate permits for each of the filming locations? What is the lead time for permit applications? How much do the permits cost? Do you have an alternative if the permits don't come through?

5. **Eyes on the ground**. If you are filming specific items or landmarks at the location, have you got confirmation that they are situated where you are expecting them? Do you have a local contact who can be your eyes on the ground, or can you recce the location yourself?

If you're filming abroad, you will most likely be working with a fixer. A fixer is someone who is based in the filming location, speaks the language, understands the filming environment, manages the permit/paperwork processes, and will accompany you and the crew on the shoot itself. Good fixers are extremely valuable.

Once you know which country you want to film in, check with the PM if they know a fixer there – it's likely they'll have already built up a network of fixer contacts. With the PM's approval and permission, contact the fixer and brief them on your planned filming dates and desired locations. The fixer will then advise on costs, permits and any other relevant information – e.g. dates on which certain locations are closed. It's best to start this conversation early, even if your plans evolve significantly – fixers will be used to this and won't be offended or upset, plus permit processing may have a long lead time in their country so it is best to give the fixers as much notice as possible.

While your own production team will book the flights and accommodation, the fixer will be responsible for supplying transport, arranging lunches and suggesting restaurants for evening meals. They accompany the crew the entire time, acting as a translation service and solving any problems on the ground for you – often seamlessly taking care of complex issues without you even knowing there was a problem in the first place! Fixers may also be able to help with local crew, such as a second camera, runner, soundie or driver. It is best to take advantage of these arrangements as local knowledge can be invaluable and local crew is often cheaper. Fixers really are fabulous, so make sure you and your crew always treat them with respect and kindness.

Scripts and beat sheets

It is unlikely you will have full control of the script at AP level – this is the PD's responsibility. However, you may be responsible for updating it, or helping the PD flesh out some aspects. You may also have the opportunity to write beat sheets, particularly if you are brought onto a project before a PD. This section will give you some guidelines on how to write beat sheets – if you're interested in scripting, take a look at Chapter 7.

A beat sheet should be between two and three pages long and should be the intermediate stage between a detailed treatment and a script. It should outline the key beats of the storyline and contain suggestions for the visuals or contributors, without being too prescriptive – it should allow room for expansion, development and creativity on the part of the director.

Beat sheets are often given to producers and directors as the basis for their full script. They should comprise a clear idea of the story, including structure, characters, locations, props, archive, need for drama reconstruction, pivotal moments, twists and, finally, payoff. It's a lot, but the discipline of creating a well thought through beat sheet will provide you with invaluable experience when it comes to the art of powerful storytelling, as well as writing a fully worked-through script.

As with many things in television, there is no definitive method for writing a good beat sheet. In this section you'll find three examples of how to do it – perhaps try each method and see which works for you.

Zenia's method

I like the five-point story method. A good story should have character development – at least one character in your story should be in a different place at the end than they were in the beginning. This could involve a physical relocation or a significant emotional development.

A great story begins *in medias res*, or right at the heart of the action. This draws the audience into the narrative immediately and makes them curious. The next part of the story needs to explain the background to this action – to place that main event in a context that emotionally engages the audience.

The third beat is a twist. Something happens, or some information is supplied, that will potentially change the initially established course of the story, the goal to which it is aiming. This then needs to be resolved before we reach the end, the final beat of the story.

Table 5.1 outlines the five story beats and three examples of stories that follow this format.

These are just the basic story beats – there is a lot more information that can be filled out between them. I tend to boil down my five story points from the research and structure the rest of the information around these main points.

Dermot's method

Experienced EP Dermot Caulfield once taught me the following method for outlining a story: the MIQ, or Main Intentional Question method.

First, establish your key story beats (as above), then next to each beat, add a question that the beat should answer. If you pull together all the MIQs in the episode, you should have a clear summary of what information will be conveyed in that episode. The next step is to identify the conflict in each beat, as well as the conflict for the overall episode.

Next to each MIQ, you should then write a summary of what will happen in that story beat. Who are the characters? What will you see? What will they say? Where are the locations?

This method adds extra elements to the storyline and creates a strong blueprint for when you come to fleshing out the script.

Table 5.1 Three stories in the five-beat structure

Beat	Story 1: Painting Freedom	Story 2: Life on Mars	Story 3: The King is Dead
Main Event	Yazidi women are painting their portraits	A spaceship is launching	The King is dead
Background	They survived ISIS captivity	The spaceship is looking for life on Mars	Was the King murdered?
Twist	They have never painted before	The astronauts don't know if they will get back alive	The King's sister wants to seize the throne
Next development	The paintings are exhibited at the Houses of Parliament	The spaceship computer starts malfunctioning	The King's brother beats the sister to the coronation
End	The paintings inspire government officials to provide aid to the women	The astronauts fix the computer and make it to Mars	The new King banishes his sister to Corsica

Interview: Jeremy Turner's method

As a director I've been given any number of beat sheets from story producers, and the one thing that I need more than anything from a Factual TV beat sheet is reality. The truth. Facts to be checked and double-checked. Being presented with a rollercoaster ride of a story might make for a good read, but if some of the beats are incorrect or, worse, completely made up, then any subsequent scripts will also be wrong and this can lead to huge problems further down the production line, as well as potentially distressing situations with contributors if you are making films of a sensitive nature. Production schedules are shorter than ever, with the knock-on effect that there is less time to write and fully fact-check beat sheets. Mistakes can happen, so if you're not 100% sure about something, just flag those facts as 'more research needed'; it will save a lot of extra stress in the long run.

The main job of a beat sheet is to provide an easy way to see if the overall story is working without getting bogged down in too many details. To do this effectively, I would suggest the first step is to work out the thesis of the film. For certain subjects – say, true crime – this should be relatively straightforward (a crime is committed, will/ how did law enforcement catch the perpetrator?); for more abstract subjects, finding a coherent argument is often easier said than done. (For the BBC show *Light Fantastic*, the thesis for the first episode was 'how our religious fascination with light drove our scientific understanding of light'). Given the pressure we are all under to get things out as quickly as possible, this step may appear a luxury, but if you can get to a clear proposition early, it will make writing everything else that follows a lot easier, because you only need to include those beats that fit the argument.

Having worked out what the point of the film is, the next stage is to get the story skeleton down. The way I like to do this is to work out what the opening scene is, then what the final scene is. Then fill in all the middle bits. There are a couple of reasons I do this. One is practical: by knowing what has changed from the beginning to the end of the story, I find it easier to chart the journey of the subject, the presenter and/or the contributors. The other is emotional: 'blank page syndrome' is a thing; at one time or another we will all experience writer's block. The best way I have found of getting around this is to work out the end of the story early on. By knowing the end of the journey I find it a lot easier to work out the best route of getting there. That's not to say the end (or the start, or the other bits) won't change along the way as the story develops, but it certainly helps me begin the trip.

The level of detail of the beats tends to increase with each draft. But I'd highly recommend starting the first draft with the minimum of information. This is part of the initial beat sheet I did for a show called *Race to Change*:

1. *Formula E – an innovative mix of old (single open-seater racing) and new (all electric)*
2. *Formula E comes to the Kingdom of Saudi Arabia (London meeting??)*
3. *The Heroes*
4. *GO!*
5. *Noha briefs the government*
6. *Choosing a location for the track*
7. *Why does oil rich KSA want electric racing? – Vision 2030*
8. *Track design*
9. *Adwa plays football – changing face of women in KSA*
10. *Music concert – more logistical nightmares*
11. *Problems building the circuit...*
12. *Extreme security measures*
13. *Track update*
14. *Bringing the world to KSA*
15. *Time really is running out*

By just keeping to the headlines, you can quickly reorder the beats to create the most compelling way to tell the story. Once you're happy with the order, you can then unpack the beats further.

For me, the next stage is to add the links in and out of the headlines and to answer the key questions of where, when, what, who, why and how. The reason I ask these question in this particular order is a result of writing drama scripts, where there is a prescriptive way of laying them out, and I find this order helps me organise my thoughts both narratively and logistically.

This is a more developed beat from a show called *Speed*:

LINK IN: Overcoming Earth's gravitational pull starts with the story of one man's audacious dream to reach for the stars, a pioneering American called Robert Goddard.

3. ROBERT GODDARD – ROCKET MAN:

Location: ROSWELL, NM, or PAKACHOAG GOLF COURSE, AUBURN, MA.

When: Could film in June/July.

What to see: Goddard's 60 ft modified tower is still present in Roswell, NM. It is just made of plain angle iron. His workshop and other historic items are on display as well.

> *Expert: SR (PRESENTER) meet XXXX rocket historian and Goddard expert.*
>
> - *Tell the highs and lows of Goddard's fascination with rockets*
> - *Can we recreate one of Goddard's rocket tests?*
>
> *LINK OUT: The space race begins.*
>
> Once you've completed the beat sheet, reread it a few times. Dig down into what you've written. Are the facts correct? Are the main story points in the most intriguing order? Told by the best person? Illustrated in the most interesting way? Is the ending satisfying? Is the ambition achievable with the time and money available?
>
> The more you are able to answer yes, the easier it will be to turn the beat sheet into a shooting script everyone can be confident in.

Once you have written the beat sheets, cast the contributors and booked the locations, you get into the more specific aspects of shoot prep. This next section will take you through these.

Interview packs

Whether you're interviewing contributors in a controlled studio-style environment or out and about on location, you'll need to prepare them packs. As mentioned on p.75, try not to send them the interview questions beforehand, but make sure they are prepped for you and your director.

Question writing is a skill that is developed over time and with practice. You should phrase questions in a way that is open-ended enough for the contributor to speak in their own words, while also targeted enough to elicit the answer you're looking for in your script. You should go through the script, identify all the information that needs to be supplied by contributors, and write questions that you think should lead to that information in their answer. Try phrasing these questions in a few different ways – perhaps write a couple of options for the director to choose from.

At this stage, you should have an idea of which contributors are best suited to which questions. You'll then need to tailor your master question sheet to the individual expertise of each contributor. Some structure their questions as tables, others as lists. It depends entirely on you or your director's preference!

Question writing is usually the task of a more experienced AP. If you are looking to gain experience or step up, asking your director if you can help by writing the interview questions is a great way to advance your skills.

For the final pack, you will need to print:

- Research notes
- Interview questions
- Script
- Shot list if you're shooting B-Roll (GVs and cutaways) or sequences as well as the sit-down interview

Make sure you add this checklist to your overall shoot checklist.

Schedules

Once you have a filming window and some details on contributor and location availability, you can start to put together a filming schedule. This will be a collaborative effort with the PM, the other APs (if there are any) and the PD(s).

The schedule is an organic entity: it will shift and shrink and grow and split right up to the last minute. So when you draw up your schedule, make sure that the formatting is easy to change. Work with the other members of the team to find a system to coordinate all the different factors you are juggling in the schedule. Whichever system you use, however technologically advanced, the key to success is communication with the rest of the team. You will need to have an excellent communication system to make sure everyone has all the up-to-date information. This can be as simple as a very active Teams chat, a whiteboard chart or a shared Excel spreadsheet.

Once the filming schedule is locked, you will need to confirm dates and times with all the different factors you are juggling: contributors, crew and locations.

Call sheets

The call sheet is ultimately the responsibility of the PM or PC, but as an AP you will have input on it. If it is a small or short-staffed production, you may take on many of the responsibilities of a PC.

The call sheet is the most important document on any production. It contains the contact details of all the relevant figures on the production, as well as emergency contacts, location details, accommodation details and the rough filming schedule. The PM will supply you with a call sheet template that already includes information such as the production's insurance company and kit list, but you will need to fill in the contact details of contributors, location specifics and the approximate schedule. Make sure you update the call sheet if there are any last-minute changes.

The PM will then send out the call sheet to all crew before the shoot, along with the risk assessment. Even if you think you know what is on it,

Figure 5.1 Shoot Folders.

make sure you read it. If you have not had any input into the call sheet, then it is even more important that you read it.

Now that the call sheet has been completed and sent out, it's time for the day of reckoning – the shoot! This next section will detail what responsibilities you have as an AP during a shoot.

Responsibilities on a shoot

Your primary purpose as an AP on a shoot is to make the PD's job as smooth as possible, especially if they are a self-shooting PD. If you have a crew with you, then the same rule applies but with more people to think about – you need to make their jobs run as smoothly as possible, because they are the ones curating and capturing the material required to create the final piece of television material.

My method for staying on top of everything during a complicated shoot is to create daily folders. I get a large pack of clear A4 sealable folders and label them with each filming day. Into each folder I put anything that is specifically needed for that day, such as props, permit documents or interview packs – at least two copies of each. I then print out three copies of the script, three copies of the risk assessment and three copies of the call sheet, one of which I mark as mine and label up with any additional details. I also create another 'admin' folder with all the release forms and insurance documents. After each shoot day is complete, I simply transfer my call sheet and script to the folder for the new day – that way I know I have everything I need on me, and I can leave any superfluous paperwork back at the hotel (see Figure 5.1).

The night before you go on a shoot, before you leave the office, double-check with the director and PM to make sure you have all the documents you need. You don't want to get to the airport and find out that you don't have the necessary carnet documents for the camera kit!

Now that you've set off on your shoot, in no particular order, these are the important things you will need to consider.

- **Fixer liaison**
  If you are filming abroad, it is likely you will be working with a fixer to set up the shoot. It is your responsibility as an AP to cultivate that relationship and liaise with the fixer to solve any problems that come up during the shoot – such as access restrictions, issues with timing, travel problems etc. They will have the local contacts to solve the problems directly, but you have the editorial oversight, so you can advise on what the best solution might be from an editorial perspective. For example, I was working on one shoot where at the last minute we discovered we did not have access to

a significant archaeological site. The fixer made some suggestions about alternatives; the editorial side (the director and I) had to come up with an another solution that would work for the story, then the fixer made the necessary arrangements to make it possible for us to film it.

- **Phone**

    Make sure you have roaming turned on. If it costs you extra, the production company can pay if you provide the PM with a receipt. Some production companies provide you with a local SIM, so it helps to have a dual-SIM phone. You will need to have internet connection to look things up on the go; you'll need minutes to call the fixer or the production team, local contacts or contributors; you'll need to be the one updating the team in the office on the go, even if it's as simple as 'shoot going well, starting scene 5'.

- **Money**

    Just like when you were a runner, you will be provided with a float by the production company (although this float will likely be a lot more!). As usual, keep the money in a clear plastic wallet and make sure you get receipts for everything. I always pack envelopes for every day of the shoot and put each day's receipts into an envelope before I go to bed, mark it with the date, then file it into the relevant folder. This makes subsequent expensing and accounting much easier. You may also be given a company card – make sure you memorise the PIN or keep it as a note in a safe place. Use the float wherever possible and only use the card for major unforeseen expenses (which you should always check with the PM before paying). If you are working with a fixer, they will invoice large expenses directly to the production company, but there may be day-to-day costs that you will need to reimburse from the float. The fixer should provide you with receipts for all of these expenses, either at the end of each day or at the end of the shoot, which you should keep in your folders or envelopes. If it is common in that country for, ahem, 'additional payments' to be made to individuals to help facilitate access, then make sure you pre-agree with your PM how you will file these expenses. The fixer will take care of such overheads, but you will of course need to reimburse them and mark up a receipt or note accordingly. It is also your responsibility to pay for any drinks, meals and additional hotel expenses for all crew, including fixers and drivers, on the shoot. If you leave a tip, make sure you note down the amount, label it as a tip and add it to your envelope of receipts.

- **Timing**
  Remember that schedule you wrote? You are also now the one responsible for making sure everyone sticks to it. There is never enough time on a shoot, no matter how much contingency you allow! You have to be disciplined and stick to schedule, otherwise the production loses money paying the crew overtime. Make sure the team is sticking within allocated hours for each sequence you need to film. If something happens outside the team's control that loses you time, see if you can make it up later. It's also wise to be a little more lenient with timekeeping in the morning, while everyone is getting into their stride, then be firmer in the afternoon. Gentle reminders to the director, such as 'we've only allowed another 15 minutes to shoot this scene' or 'we need to be leaving for the next location in an hour', are sufficient.

- **Cross-referencing**
  As the team is shooting, make sure you're cross-referencing everything with the script and the schedule. If you get time during the prep, you may even find it helpful to create a document that outlines the schedule, the script for the section you're shooting and the shot list all in one handy place. Before you leave a location, take some time to double-check the script and shot list and make sure you've covered everything you're supposed to in that location.

- **Food & water**
  Keep an eye out for everyone's energy levels. A hungry crew is a mutinous crew. If you're shooting abroad, the fixer should be able to help with supplying snacks and drinks, but if it's just you, then you will need to make sure everyone has coffee in the morning, water throughout the day and lunch at an appropriate time. This is particularly important if you are filming in extreme environments.

- **Health & Safety**
  This is ultimately the responsibility of the director, who will have signed off the risk assessment, but you should keep an eye out for it too. You should be supplied with a small first aid kit by the production team – make sure it's in your rucksack at all times. The call sheet should also list the person on the crew who is a trained first-aider – if that's not you, make sure you know who it is. If you're not sure about something, err on the side of caution. For example, I was on a shoot in Egypt and the director's ankle swelled up to an alarming size. It didn't hurt but equally it didn't look right. I decided to call it and ask the fixer to take her to hospital – fortunately, it was just a nasty insect bite and she was given

antibiotics. I had to write out an incident report and inform the production team – but in the end everyone was safe.

- **Contributor/presenter care**

  Just as you were the first point of contact for the contributors while setting up the shoot, so you will be their primary 'carer' during the shoot. When they arrive, make sure they are greeted and introduced to everyone, that they feel settled and have all the information they need. During the shoot, especially if they are new talent, make sure they are comfortable with the schedule, and that any requests or needs are met – just like the crew, make sure they are fed and watered.

- **DIT (Department of IT)**

  Unless you have a dedicated crew member who will back up the rushes (shot footage), this will likely fall to you. Every production company has their own preferred system for backing up and labelling rushes – make sure you go through this with the production team before you go on the shoot. Some simply copy-paste the folders from the cards and then rename them manually; others prefer to use software such as ShotPut. You will need to back up to both the master and the backup drives. It is best practice to do each drive individually, as opposed to copying to one and then copying the backed-up files to another drive. Doing each drive individually avoids copying corrupted files. Make sure you are supplied with firebolt connectors for the fastest copying speed and that your laptop has enough ports to copy to two drives simultaneously – otherwise you'll be there for hours. If the production company tries to give you a laptop that doesn't have enough ports, ask for an extender or kick up a stink. You are well within your rights to do this, as some members of the production team don't know just how exhausting shoots are and how much time it takes to back up. You need your sleep so make sure the backup doesn't take longer than it needs to. The production company should supply you with enough 'stock' (cards – specific to each type of camera) and card readers. Check the card readers before you leave for the shoot. I once got on a shoot and discovered the card reader didn't work. We had shot 8 hours of footage that day. The production company sent out a spare with a contributor, but in the meantime, we had to copy to the laptop's hard drive, which only had enough memory for half the footage! It was a rather panicky day, fortunately solved by some great communication and planning from the production team. However, if I had checked the card reader before travelling, we wouldn't have had that problem…

The edit: sync pull

It is rare for APs to be kept on until the edit, but if you are, it is likely you will be asked to do a sync pull. This involves going through interview transcripts from contributors and pulling out the useful sections. Ask your director if they have a preference for how you should organise this – sometimes directors like to arrange by topic or script section; some like you to highlight in different colours. You will want to over-pull to start with; then this will be refined down to bitesize, snappy lines that build the body of the programme. This is a great way to get experience that will lead to an edit-producing job.

Casting AP: interview with Mitch Langcaster-James

Casting is one of the most fundamental jobs in television. At the heart of most unscripted TV shows is a 'contributor', whether it be a talent show auditionee, a game show contestant or the next reality TV star. TV is designed to entertain and tell a story, which is very hard to do without brilliant contributors. It's the responsibility of the casting team on any show to hunt down these amazing people, find out what the story is and tell it in an entertaining but responsible way. Being a casting AP is also one of the most employable roles in the TV industry. TV shows constantly need fresh faces and so casting APs are usually working all year round to find them.

I've cast everything from daytime gardening programmes to popular studio shows, hard-hitting documentaries to big-budget reality. To work in casting you fundamentally need to be personable, but everything else is just tips and tricks you can pick up along the way. There are a few key stages when it comes to approaching any casting job: it really helps to get your head around these early on. You need to find out exactly who you're looking for, figure out where you're going to find these people, know how to approach them and then, assuming they want to participate, successfully be able to pitch them to more senior producers to get them on the show.

Thoroughly understand the brief

As early on as possible, you need to try to establish a clear idea of exactly what the show you're working on is looking for. This isn't always as easy as it sounds. It might be a first series and the team aren't yet sure exactly what contributors (usually referred to as 'contribs') they'll need. It may even be that they're waiting to see what contributors you find to see how that might steer the show; it can be a delicate balancing act. However, if it's a returning series, or the team have a clear vision of what they want, it's best to get your head around this straight away. What age range are they looking for? Do they need to be from a specific location? Should they have had a certain life experience? Be from a specific background or own a certain item? Whatever it is, get as much information as you can early on, write it all down and start trying to think about how you're going to get access to the kind of person or people who would fit the brief. If it's a returning show, watch as many previous episodes as you can. If it's a new series, ask to see the 'treatment', which outlines what the production company are hoping to make the show about. The more you understand the features and characteristics of the contributors who are needed, the easier they'll be to find.

Where are you going to find these people?

Finding your contributors is arguably the core task of a casting AP's job and is also usually the hardest part. Once you have a clear picture in your mind of the kind of people you're on the hunt for, you need to figure out how you're going to actually find them – in casting it's usually called 'targeting'. There are different approaches to targeting contributors, some more time-consuming than others, and it can depend on the kind of person you're looking for as to what approach you'll take.

Social media

Today, social media has become an increasingly important tool for casting and it is now used as at least a base-level approach to casting on the vast majority of TV shows. As a casting AP, on day one I usually tried to get my social media plan in place. The wording of casting materials can be key – good writing can bring in just the right people, but say the wrong thing and you'll end up with an empty application inbox. I would write out any adverts I might want to post and get it all signed off by a senior member of the team as early as possible. Most casting APs will have designated social media casting accounts, which they keep separate from any personal accounts. It allows you to post online or contact people directly, while holding on to your own privacy, which is important. So, if you've managed to land yourself your first casting gig, setting up some work accounts straight away is a good idea.

Social media can be a really brilliant tool for advertising to a specific group of people. Thanks to savvy algorithms on platforms like Facebook, you can cheaply post an advert and choose for it to be shown to only people of a certain age range, with specific interests, who own pets, or have a specific job, for example. For a popular returning series, it may be that they can use social media in this way to advertise that they are accepting applications again and watch the contributors just come rolling in. However, most shows aren't that lucky and I found that the best contributors come from a more proactive approach.

Proactive promotion

It's best to not just rely on a simple social media campaign if possible. If initial adverts or generic posts aren't giving you much to work with, it's important to crack on with being more proactive and spreading the word far and wide. Being proactive can still involve the use of social media – for example, if you're looking for green-fingered folk in need of some help with their gardens, there are countless Facebook groups you can join filled with garden lovers where you might find someone. Being more proactive might just also take you down the route of approaching gardening magazines and negotiating shoutouts or setting up a call with a regional village planting group.

If you're looking to target a certain demographic, one approach often used involves finding people by the sorts of places they might frequent. For example, if you were casting youngsters from Manchester for a dating reality show, think about the kind of venues potential contributors might visit in the city. Chances are you're looking for people who are young, fun, up for a good time and happy to put themselves out there in public. Start by trying to ascertain – are there any local Instagram hotspots? Restaurants whose cocktails are always all over social media? Iconic landmarks where wannabe influencers are always taking their pictures? A quick search by location on Instagram, or looking on Facebook for those who have 'checked in' to a specific cocktail bar, can give you a great list of people who may well be in the right demographic for what you're looking for.

Active casting

'Active casting' is a term that can get thrown around when you're on a casting team. Sometimes if a producer says they want to see 'active casting', it just means that they don't want the team to solely rely on social media and they expect people to get out there as much as possible. However, some shows genuinely require an incredibly 'active', direct, targeted form of casting – the nitty gritty task of finding niche groups or those standout contributors who can make an entire series a success.

In the past, I have had to cast some very specific individuals with very niche characteristics. Let's say, for example, that you're casting for a new documentary which aims to highlight the challenges young people with social anxiety face and you've been tasked with finding young men who struggle to leave their own home. A key part of being a casting AP is putting yourself in the shoes of the person you're looking for. Think of it like being a detective. In the first instance it'll help you find them, but it'll also help you to relate to them, further down the line.

If you're looking for someone specific, like those who are housebound, you might want to first of all consider what this person's life might actually be like on an average day. Start with what hobbies they might have. If you're looking for young guys stuck at home, who want to keep entertained, there's a good chance they could be into gaming. Once you get to that assumption, figure out where you might find a committed gamer who likes to chat. A good dig around online will tell you what the best forums and discussion platforms are for hardcore gamers. With permission from the site, this could be a great place to start posting adverts and letting users know who you're looking for. You'll need to come up with multiple approaches like this, but take each one at a time. For example, now you've got the word out there in gaming communities, what sorts of things are young guys eating who can't leave the house? Chances are they could be relying quite a lot on take-out food if they're not able to eat out, so your next job becomes to find a group of people who perhaps like a particular take-out service, and so on. With methods like this, you'll find yourself more likely to be promoting to the specific kinds of individuals you actually need, without relying on them just stumbling upon your social media post.

How to approach people

Approaching people to appear on TV shows should always be done sensitively. Depending on the programme, hearing from a member of the casting team might be a really exciting time for the contributor, so you may need to manage their expectations in case they don't make it onto the show. Similarly, if you're casting a show which tackles a particularly sensitive subject, it's vital to approach things with the utmost care. Much like getting sign-off for any adverts you may want to post, it can be good practice to draft the message you plan to use when approaching individuals and get this signed off first by the most senior member of the casting team. You'll never be able to know everything there is to know about every community, but certain terms and phrases might be deemed offensive or insensitive and you don't realise it. It's best to always check.

Pitching your contributors

Congratulations, you've found the dream contributor! It was a difficult brief, but you've managed to track down the perfect person. You even managed to do it in an innovative way and you're feeling chuffed. You think they're a great character with an even better story, but the next challenge is being able to get your casting producer or SP to see this too. This is where pitching comes in. When you're a casting AP you'll often have one or two pitch meetings a week. This is your time to sell your contributors and explain why you think they're perfect for the show.

Casting tapes
You can write the best description of what someone is like and what their story is, but nothing will ever compare to hearing someone tell you in their

own words what they've been through. As a result, it is now common to use casting tapes to help with a pitch. This involves having a video call with a contributor you like and recording it, before editing it down into a short tape which should show off all the best things about that contributor. It gives a flavour of their personality, their emotions, their confidence on camera and is a brilliant indicator of what they could be like, should they make it onto the show. It can be a hard task, but a brilliant casting AP is someone who can produce a tape which perfectly captures a contributor's character, while also including any important information for the show they're applying for. The trick is to then also produce a tape that will appeal to the person you're pitching to.

If you're hoping to get a job on a casting team or if you've secured your first role and you're a bit nervous about it, practice makes perfect. All you need to do is get your hands on some basic video editing software. There are free ones you can use online, or most computers these days will come with some sort of editing tool you can use. Before my first role, I would download random 30-minute interviews from YouTube, which talked about different topics. I would then task myself with cutting these down to 10-minute, 5-minute and then 60-second casting tapes, trying to sell the person as much as possible. As with all things, you get quicker and quicker at doing it. You become more confident using the software and more adept at knowing which are the best lines to keep and which can be cut. Cutting casting tapes is an incredibly useful skill to have, so the more you do it, the better you'll be at your job.

Contributor welfare

In the past, there have been accusations of some TV shows not always treating their contributors with enough care. In recent years, it's been brilliant to see more emphasis put on contributor welfare and your part in this should start from the moment you first approach someone. Thankfully, lots of production companies these days have a welfare service provider on board to help support contributors. This is especially vital if you're casting for a programme which might highlight a mental health issue or difficult life scenario, as you may be working with potentially vulnerable individuals. It can also be a good idea to look into mental health training for yourself, so you know you're doing the very best for your contributors that you possibly can.

Alongside this, just remember to always be polite, professional and understanding, as this is likely to be a new and nerve-wracking experience for people you contact. Casting inevitably requires some flexibility – for example, your contributor may only be able to chat to you in the evening, when you're supposed to have finished working for the day. But where possible, keep clear professional boundaries when finding out more about your contributors. If they're a similar age or personality type to you, it can be easy for conversations to feel very friendly, but it's important to keep in mind at all times why you're talking to them and not to allow professional boundaries to become blurred.

Most shows have what's colloquially called 'the talk of doom'. It refers to an open and honest discussion with contributors about the worst-case scenario they might experience, should they take part in your project. It's important to be totally transparent as to what is involved in taking part in your show, so people can give their informed consent. If you have any concerns about a contributor taking part, make sure you flag these straight away.

Mental health in TV is being talked about more and more, as it should be. Often, the casting team will find themselves doing a lot more than just finding people to go on TV. You frequently become a source of support throughout a contributor's time on a show and it's important to always be on the lookout for anyone struggling. We want to find brilliant characters to put on TV, but make sure we're doing so responsibly. At the end of the day, being on TV should always be a fun and positive experience.

Shooting AP: interview with Mitch Langcaster-James

Arguably, one of the most demanding roles in television is being a shooting AP. A shooting AP needs to be creative, with the people skills of a producer, but also have the technical camera knowledge and artistic eye of a camera operator. However, trying to juggle both a creative and technical role at once, with a heavy camera on your shoulder, can be a real challenge.

As budgets get tighter and crews get smaller, shows are increasingly looking for 'self-shooters' to come on board. This essentially means they're looking for an AP who is able to come up with content and also film it themselves. As a shooting AP you might be both producing and filming a key interview, acting as the second camera alongside a more experienced shooter or even shooting an entire sequence on your own. Of course, shooting will come a bit more instinctively to some people, but I'm a firm believer that anyone can learn how to shoot to a broadcast standard, with enough time and the right support. The tricky part can be getting your hands on the equipment in the first instance. Production companies usually hire in camera equipment and will rarely be paying for it to just sit around. Experienced shooters will always need the kit to be available for the tasks at hand, so it can be a challenge to get the initial experience. However, there are a number of ways you can make it happen and pick up vital skills.

You don't need to have studied media, or get a degree, to work in television by any means, though some people do choose to study first out of personal preference. One of the main benefits to studying some TV courses is that they can guarantee you hands-on time with camera and sound equipment, which can sometimes make things easier if you know you're going to want to shoot professionally. Alternatively, some people choose to work in a 'kit house' for a while. Kit houses are companies which own and rent out camera equipment to be used on productions. It's a common place to start for those who want to become traditional camera operators as you get the time and exposure to really learn the ins and outs of the technology behind the camera kit. Some people do then make the jump from the kit house to being an AP and bring their shooting knowledge with them. It's also possible to try to just learn on the job and pick up skills as you go, which is a route more and more people are going down.

Some people in the TV industry specifically seek out a shooting role and know they want to go down that route from the start. However, it's also not uncommon to find yourself being thrown in at the deep end and having a camera thrust into your hand without much notice. I'm not ashamed to say that I definitely fell into the latter category. I had been thinking for some time that shooting might be something I wanted to explore, but I wasn't actively pursuing it. I found myself working on an observational documentary which followed individuals travelling to a new hotel in the Caribbean and I was due to fly in and out of the UK with the contributors. With the rest of the film crew permanently based abroad, they needed someone who could film the contributors at the airport before taking off. Having previously mentioned in passing that I might be interested in learning to shoot at some point, it quickly became my time to shine! My baptism of fire into self-shooting ended up with me getting a quick 35-minute lesson from a member of the crew, in the back of a dark taxi on the way to Gatwick Airport, at midnight – not ideal! After only 3 and a half hours' sleep, I was interviewing and shooting at the same time, all by myself, in a Gatwick terminal, desperately trying to remember everything I'd learned the night before. Thankfully, the footage ended up being usable, and from then on I began shooting regularly on the show and found my confidence grew pretty rapidly.

This experience proved to be invaluable, and luckily for me, straight after this show I was snapped up to go and be the shooting AP on the reboot of a well-known food show. With only a limited amount of experience, I had the basics of how to shoot, but not the style and flair of someone with proper training. Although there's no better way to learn than by just doing the job, I signed up to a free online 'Basics of Shooting' course, to help me get up to speed in the meantime, which I would encourage anyone to do. I was fortunate that my new series director was incredibly supportive, and, knowing I was new to shooting, really took the time to make sure I was learning the technical nitty gritty, while having the space to experiment and try things out visually for myself. The reality is that when it comes to shooting, there might not always be a perfect moment to learn, and sometimes you do need to make the most of a tricky situation. If it's an appropriate time to do so, always let people know on your team if shooting is something you're interested in. If there's a quiet moment between takes, ask your PD if you can watch them work over their shoulder. If a shooting AP is struggling with their equipment, offer to help carry their kit, and take the opportunity to ask about it as you go. It might take a bit of luck to find the right time, but sometimes just letting people know you're keen to learn is the first hurdle.

There are a few basic shots you'll need to get your head around if you're looking to start shooting. Let's say you've been asked to go and film a celebrity chef working at their restaurant. To shoot in the simplest form, you'd typically start by shooting GVs, short for 'General Views'. These are the context shots that establish where you are – in this case, it might be the camera panning to the outside of the restaurant. You'll then have your primary footage, which is sometimes referred to as 'actuality' depending on what you're covering. This is the raw footage showing events unfolding – in this case, the chef cooking a specific recipe. To go alongside this, you'd shoot 'cutaways'. Cutaways are supplementary shots which cut away from the main action to something more specific going on, and also give you an alternative visual to work with when you're in the edit. They can be particularly helpful when some audio has been captured that's useful but the visuals aren't ideal. In this scenario, you'd film tighter shots of just the chef's hands chopping ingredients, turning on the oven or opening a cupboard. Lastly, you'd shoot B-Roll, which describes all the other footage that isn't the primary action. This could be something simple like the chef setting the table, ready for the meal to be served. It gives you something relevant to see other than just non-stop cooking and can also be used to cover up any creative editing you're having to do with the main footage.

There are lots of other shots you'll need to master to be able to shoot at a high level, but a basic knowledge like this should get you going. Fortunately, you don't need a state-of-the-art television camera these days to have a go at the basics. With a standard smartphone, you can start filming and putting together practice content which will put you in good stead for when you start shooting professionally. After my first experience shooting, when I was trying to improve, I decided to challenge myself by filming short VTs using just my phone. I would 'interview' a willing friend, shoot my own GVs and cutaways, even writing a little voiceover script. If you then try to edit the footage down, you can often see where you might have gone wrong. It'll highlight which shots you might have missed, the questions you should have asked or the shots that didn't look as good as you thought they would. Starting to get your head around this early on will really help when you start learning to actually shoot.

If you manage to land your first shooting gig, take some time to properly critique and analyse television that has already been made. Watch a popular property programme or cooking show and think critically about how they frame their shots, how they focus the camera and the lighting effects they use to change the mood. You'll find that when you watch with a critical eye, certain shows are actually quite formulaic. Different shows have different styles – some documentaries might be quite artistic and alternative, which you'll notice is a world apart from how a standard news interview is set up. Incorporate as many of these techniques as you can into your different practice VTs and you should be able to see obvious improvements before you've even started your new job.

If you're out on location, being a shooting AP doesn't just mean producing a contributor and holding a camera; chances are you will also have to think about lighting and sound. It's impossible to know everything there is to know about every single department; that's why specialist sound and lighting directors exist. But to be a shooting AP, you'll need a good working knowledge of the bare essentials. You'll need to learn how to set up a radio microphone and make sure it's on the same frequency as the receiver. You'll have to know how to put together a panel light and make sure the temperature (warmth of the light, measured in kelvins) is right for the space. All of this can be picked up as you go along, but read up on as much of it as you can ahead of time.

Despite being such a challenging role, being a shooting AP can also be unbelievably satisfying. There's no greater thrill than sitting down with your friends and family to watch a mainstream TV show and being able to point out a scene that you shot yourself. Knowing that you were not only the one holding the camera, but you also lit the space, captured the sound and even managed to both find and produce the contributor all yourself, is incredibly rewarding. It's not a simple role, but with practice it becomes more and more manageable and is a fantastic string to have to your bow when working in the TV industry.

Summary

- Be extremely organised – this is the number one top quality of a good AP
- Start to think like a director – anticipate the needs of the production
- It is worth spending a little longer in this role to learn as many skills and variations as possible

What to watch

As soon as I became an AP, I started mentally costing up every scene I watched in a drama or a documentary. I started evaluating contributors and making notes of good ones. I started looking out for inconsistencies in interview backgrounds or shot styles. I started counting the number of setups. It made me a very annoying partner with whom to watch TV, but these are all good habits to keep your brain in the game when you're watching TV as well as making it. At this stage in your career, you may have less time to watch TV – but when you do, pause and think about all the different elements that went into every shot. I particularly recommend watching the *Storyville* series on the BBC or hit Netflix documentaries such as *Tiger King* or *Making a Murderer* – the craftmanship of these series in terms of sourcing material and contributors and weaving them together over a long period of time into an edge-of-your-seat documentary is the peak of documentary-making skill.

Chapter 6

Producer

This role is very similar to that of the assistant producer (AP), but with greater financial oversight and editorial guidance. Even if a director is brought in for the actual shoot, the producer is the ultimate authority on the overall narrative and story.

Not all productions have producers. In fact, the staffing balance on a production is entirely at the discretion of the production company or even the individual exec. There is no rigid or prescriptive team structure – only tried and tested staffing formulae that have been developed in particular working environments over time. A producer is more senior than an AP, but will likely be paid less per week/day than a director – primarily because the producer's contract will usually be far longer than the director's. The director may only be brought on for the shoot or for specific script development; the producer, on the other hand, will have more contact with all the other factors that must be considered in the production – the budget, the commissioner, the editorial parameters, the overall logistics. This is why, ultimately, the producer has the final say over the production.

The most common way to step up from AP to producer is within a production company. For example, if you have a couple of roles as an AP under your belt, you should be able to ask to step up to producer if you are offered another role on a production within the company.

Another route to the producer role is via a producer director position, especially if you're keen to become an edit producer or branded content Producer – both positions in which ideally you would have some directing experience. The third way is to step up via the position of a story producer. In order to get this role, you should be a very experienced AP and be able to prove some familiarity with writing beat sheets or directing interviews.

Story producer

A story producer will tend to take on the same responsibilities as an AP but with more editorial oversight. They will likely be the person writing

DOI: 10.4324/9781003294009-7

the beat sheets and possibly even parts of the script. One docu-drama I worked on split the documentary and drama between the story producers and directors respectively. In this case, the producers and directors had to work very closely together in order to ensure a continuous and complementary narrative across the script, while developing their respective sections separately.

As a story producers, you should have nailed all the skills listed in the chapter on APs, plus a selection of directorial skills. Before you take on a story producers job, make sure you've read the chapter on Directing – that way you will be prepared to go above and beyond!

Once you have done a few story producer roles, you can easily move to branded content or step up to producer/director, if that is your planned path. For some people, however, a story producer role can be the best of both worlds – plenty of creative control over and investment in the story without the pressure of responsibility for the whole production. The skills required for a story producer translate very well to an edit producer role – although you may need to transfer via a short stint as a producer/director in order to get there.

Archive producer: interview with Emily Mayson

I don't think many archive producers start out wanting to work with archive. Most of us fall into it, taking a sidestep from being a researcher or production coordinator. A background in research is helpful. However, I have trained up a few archive researchers with limited experience but the right attitude, and they are fantastic. It's a job that you learn by doing. If you want to work in archive, you can read up on copyright law, analyse archive-heavy films or practise cutting together your own narratives from existing footage (being careful not to breach copyright if you share your work). But the best way in is to get work experience with archive producers or offer to help your archive colleagues – they'll often be glad of an extra pair of hands and can teach you a lot.

To become an archive producer, you need to become the best archive researcher you can be. Learn as much as you can about the legal and budgeting side of archive from your senior colleagues. Archive producing carries more responsibility, so you need to feel confident before you step up.

I was archive producing long before I was credited and paid as such, because I was working alone as an archive researcher. I did the work and ran everything past the production manager (PM) to check over and sign off. It gave me the freedom to learn the job without the responsibility for any potential mistakes. Various colleagues told me I should step up to archive producer, and I plucked up the courage to ask my bosses, but they said no. It eventually happened when I moved to a different company with a new PM who recognised my work and gave me the credit. By that time, I was confident in the role, so the new title and responsibility weren't too intimidating.

My experience as an archive researcher differs from that of the researchers I now work with or have trained up, as they are working as part of an archive team. They focus only on research, but have the support of an archive producer. There is value in both routes.

As an archive researcher, try to get your head round the legal and money side of things as early as possible. Then it won't feel like a massive step up to producing. Those aspects of the job are an innate part of the process for me because I've been doing it since I started. The researchers on my team primarily do archive research, but I encourage them to negotiate with suppliers, check cuts for factual inaccuracies and compliance issues, and read through contracts, even though I take ultimate responsibility for those things. They are skills that will serve them well in the future. Some of this you will learn by osmosis on the job, but be proactive in asking questions and grabbing opportunities to practise, and you will progress faster.

There are three main elements to archive producing – research, budget and legal. Research is the same as when you're an archive researcher; you just have to balance the other things at the same time! You're more likely to be doing the harder, more time-consuming research, as this becomes easier the more experienced you are. You are responsible for the archive budget and will work with the PM to balance this. Using your contacts at archive libraries, you'll make deals and work with the editors to make sure they are maximising those deals in the content they use. You can often find the same or a very similar image in a different library, so you can switch things around to replace expensive archive with cheaper options or options that are covered by bulk discounts. Lastly, you are responsible for the legal side of things – making sure you have licensing agreements in place with archive suppliers that cover the programme for all the rights that the broadcaster's contract demands. You also need to make sure the way the archive is being used is not misleading – showing the right person/place/year as the VO, presenter or interview suggests, and making sure there are no negative implications (like unintentionally suggesting that an innocent person is a criminal). One edit producer jokes that I'm 'ruining a good programme in the name of factual accuracy' – but I say I'm stopping us from getting sued!

Archive producers need to be tenacious, creative and have a keen eye for detail. You also need to be logical, organised and unafraid of spreadsheets. You need the creative vision to know what to put on screen editorially, but have the logical discipline to work with both numbers and legal documents. Insatiable curiosity is necessary in tracking down elusive archive or copyright holders. You need to be able to communicate – with your production team, with the edit teams and with the archive suppliers. You have to stay calm under pressure and be able to have your mind working across different planes (creative/logical/legal) and different episodes/narratives/series simultaneously. You need to look at the big picture of series deals and balancing a budget across the series but be able to look for the fine details like specific wording in contracts, voiceovers and image descriptions to make sure the archive can be used and is used correctly. You also need to be able to flick between doing all those things, because you never know which curveball the edit is going to throw you next! It can be a complex and unusual combination of brain gymnastics, but that's what makes the job so fun and rewarding.

A visual memory is useful. When an editor requests something you know you've already found, you know exactly where to find it. On the downside, if you're working on disturbing subject matter, it makes it hard to forget what you've seen. You have to sift through all the images that are too gruesome or distressing to show on TV. Even the innocuous history shows I work on seem to have an unexpectedly high body count!

People think I'm mad, but one of my favourite parts of the job is getting episodes down to budget. I find it thrilling. It's a bit like doing a jigsaw puzzle without the picture on the box. You're doing creative maths and creative visuals at the same time. Making deals with your contacts at archive libraries enables you to reduce the cost of the 'wallpaper' to make room in the budget for the editorially crucial shots. You work with the editor to take the show apart and put it back together with different archive. Often, they say it's better than the archive they used originally – because you know the archive and your log best and can suggest the very best shots. It's satisfying to see the total cost drop below budget, knowing that the programme's visuals are the best they can be.

Work closely with the editor and edit producer – visit them in the edit suite if you can. Get a good understanding of how their edit process works. Different editors work in different ways – some work with visuals from day one, whereas others create a solid narrative structure and then add in all the archive at the last minute. Be a real person to them and stay up to date with what they need, as their requests can change quickly. If they know you and trust your system, they are less likely to rip unclearable things from the internet and you are more likely to be able to get them exactly what they need. It's also easier to make changes for cost if you're already working closely together.

When doing initial research, always get establishing or aerial shots of locations (unless this has been filmed specially). Photos of places in the right era are helpful for historic stories. Try to get images of all characters mentioned. When reading the script for visual ideas, think about who, what, where and when. You have to 'stalk' your historical characters – find out where they lived, worked, went to school, whether they were part of any social or academic institutions. Your story might be about one part of their life, but their image might be found in another. Once I was looking for an image of a particular Victorian gentleman and discovered that, away from what he was known for, he also had a financial interest in a brewery. I got in touch with the brewery, and they had a portrait of him hanging in a back room, which they kindly photographed for me!

You also have to track people down when you find their footage or photo online without clear contact details and you need their consent to use it. This is when the skills you learned while social media stalking your best friend's crush at school come in handy! You need to master the unthreatening unsolicited message. You need to be particularly sensitive when the copyright holder has passed away and you are contacting their family for permission (copyright generally lasts for seventy years after the creator's death). Obituaries contain good leads. I once contacted someone's widow through the vicar who conducted the funeral service – she was still part of the congregation.

Another time, I needed to clear some YouTube footage and there were no contact details. The username was a nickname, not a full name. I could see from the comments that he was local to where he filmed the footage. So I rang the nearest pub and asked if they knew him. 'He's here,' they said. 'I'll pass you over.'

A good spreadsheet, log and filing system is invaluable. If you have to eye-match all the archive in a cut because it's badly labelled, it will take you days. If the EDL (Edit Decision List) is a timecoded list of filenames which contain the information you need, you know what's in the cut and what it costs before you even press play. Give each piece of archive a unique roll number in the filename that correlates with the log. The log tells you and the editors what's what to avoid factual mistakes. Automate the sums in your costing spreadsheet to avoid human error. It can take some years to develop and refine a spreadsheet that deals with this all at once in a way that works for you, but it is worth it.

Usually, we edit programmes with low-resolution archive and then get the high-resolution master version once we are sure what is in the finished programme. Getting masters in all at once can be difficult, so get as much as you can in ahead of time. I worked on a programme that needed masters from Japan, LA and Spain –there was no time zone that worked for all of them! I didn't get much sleep that week…

Archive research isn't wholly editorial or wholly production. It bridges the two, so you are both and neither. Sometimes you know more about what's going on than anyone, as you heard about it from everyone (there's a tendency to become the team therapist). Sometimes you're the last to know because people forget you as you're not attached to a particular edit team. I manage teams of archive researchers on big projects now, and it's fantastic being part of an archive team after years of being the only archive person. It can be a little lonely and feel as if no one else really understands your job. It's helpful to form alliances with other archive people on other productions at your company or at networking events. They might have ideas on where to find things or a contact at a niche library that can help.

As you get more senior, you become more influential on the final cut. Sometimes this is by being actively involved in editorial decisions when working closely with the editor or even in pre-production, when you can veto a story that's not possible to illustrate with archive. Sometimes your influence is more subtle. I realised that most of the archive that comes up first on searches is of white males. Now, as a matter of course, my team and I override the search algorithms by searching for diverse options. If the request is for scientists, we will search 'female scientist', 'Black scientist', 'Asian scientist' etc. I don't know whether the editors even notice that they are making more diverse shot choices, but we're proud that we are making better programming.

We keep learning. There are so many elements to archive and copyright law that you're never going to learn it all in one go. New projects will bring exciting new challenges, like exploring a different genre (history archive differs from crime or entertainment, for example) or getting archive from another country (which may have different copyright laws or require government permission to use archive of historical artefacts). Learn as much as you can and always refer things upwards to your PM, execs or lawyer. The next time you come across that facet of copyright law or a tricky research request, you'll know what to do.

Drama producer

This is a role you may take on if you work on a lot of drama-docs. The balance of drama to documentary can vary between productions. At one end of the scale, a little drama reconstruction is used to add value to the production or to fill in visuals when actuality is difficult to come by. At the other end of the scale, the production is mostly drama, with some expert interviews to add substance and context to the storyline. There are productions with the drama/doc balance at various points along this scale (see Figure 6.1).

If the production is more at the drama end of the scale, it's likely that you'll have a full drama crew. However, if it's half-and-half or less, you'll likely be operating with a drama reconstruction crew, which is much smaller, requires more ingenuity and much more work from the drama producer. If you've just landed a job as a drama producer, here's what you need to think about in order to ensure as smooth a production process as possible.

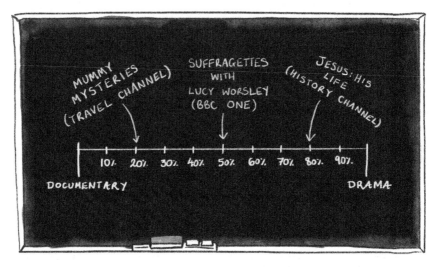

Figure 6.1 Documentary vs Drama.

1. **Break down the script**
    The director(s) will have marked sections to be filled by drama. That may just be visuals or it may include dialogue. You will need to go through this script and carefully break it down by character, setup, location, props – anything else required that is mentioned in the script. Some directors are more thorough than others in their drama sections – make sure you sit down with them and have a detailed conversation about how they see the drama sections, and most importantly, what storytelling function the drama is supposed to convey. If you are working with multiple scripts or multiple episodes, you'll need to do this for every single one, then collate your breakdown so that you can analyse what setups can be doubled up, which props can have multiple uses etc. Be prepared for these scripts to change and make sure that you have a good communications system with the director(s) so that they know to send you any updates or share any significant changes.

2. **Research**
    Now for the fun part. Once you've broken down the script, you'll need to research the context of each drama scene. Collaborate with the researcher, directors or producers to access their existing research – or better still, get them to brief you. Then supplement that with your own research. For example, what did Egyptian soldiers wear during the Ptolemaic period? What time of day

(or night) was it when Alan Turing finished the Enigma-cracking bombe? You'll need as much detail as possible so that the scene can be lit correctly, so that the set can be dressed accurately, so that the right costumes can be hired. Remember that this needs to be visual research as far as possible – perhaps create a mood board or image folders. These will be useful down the line too, when the set designers, art department and costume suppliers get involved.

3.   **Props**
In your script breakdown, make sure you note the key props that are crucial to the script. Research what they look like and if you're using a prop buyer or set designer, brief them on it in detail. If you're doing all the drama reconstruction inside a studio (see below), then you'll need a set designer who can construct the different sets you'll need and supply the props and set dressing items in bulk. However, on a location shoot (see below for more detail), it's more likely you'll have most of the things you need to build the atmosphere of the scene, and can cherry-pick your hero props.

4.   **Costumes**
Go through the script again and note down all the costumes that are required, plus any costume changes. You'll then need to create a shopping list of costume items – and note when some items can be doubled up across characters, as that'll save some money. Accessories might seem like a waste of money but they make a huge difference – make sure you fight to get those accessories within the costume budget. I worked on one show where we almost had to can a scene because we didn't have the right hat for a character.

5.   **Actors/supporting artistes**
If your drama reconstruction involves only non-speaking roles, you will likely use supporting artistes (SAs) as your cast. It is best to use an agency for this, as the booking and billing process is much easier, they are usually able to vet the SAs effectively and they can provide accurate recommendations. One of the great advantages to using an agency is that if the SA is late or, worse, doesn't turn up, they risk heavy consequences from the agency, which reduces their likelihood of messing up your production by not turning up for work! For speaking roles, you'll need to work through agents. Make sure that the actors are registered with Equity and do a proper casting call. I strongly advise conducting these casting calls in person. A director I knew once tried to do them over Skype and it didn't work out well for the overall production. The number of

speaking roles you can have may be limited by budget restrictions. In this case, you will need to work very closely with the director to figure out the best way in which their script can be brought to life within the budget constraints.

6. **Schedule**
    Once you have your cast, your scene breakdown, your costumes and your props sorted, then you have to solve the enigma of the shooting schedule. The key deciding factor will be your sets: shooting all the scenes for one particular setup while another setup is being prepared, and staggering this throughout the day in the most efficient way. Your next priority is the cast: making sure that SAs don't play two characters in the same episode, or, if they do, that their faces are not visible in one of the scenes. You'll also need to factor in enough time for costume changes. Once you have arranged these in an efficient order, then you can add the costumes and props required by your schedule for each scene and finalise the bookings for the actors and SAs.

7. **Studio shoot**
    If the drama director or series producer (SP) decides to film in a studio, there are several factors you'll need to consider when choosing your studio. Firstly, convenience. Is it close to public transport routes? Is it easy to find? You may have to pay your SAs and crew extra if they have to travel a long distance outside London (or the nearest city to which you are shooting), plus you run the risk of cast or crew getting lost and delaying your schedule. Secondly, space. Does it have enough space for all your setups? You'll want to fit at least two setups within your studio space so that the art department or set designers can be working on one while you shoot in the other. Does it have a good enough lighting rig? Does it have a workshop space for the art department and set designers? Does it have enough space for a green room, a make-up room and a costume room? Is there also enough room for men and women to change separately? What are the craft (food) options? Does the studio provide catering or will you have to bring this in separately? Can the studio provide radios? Prepare yourself a checklist based on these questions when you view studios, and make sure you write down quotes so that the PM can compare costs and facilities.

8. **Location shoot**
    Set designers hate me for this, but I infinitely prefer a location shoot to a studio shoot. What you lose in accommodation costs

you more than make up for in set construction and prop costs, as well as the quality of the overall result and look of the show. Plus (again lighting designers will hate me for this) there's only so much you can do with lighting to recreate an entire era. You'll still have similar considerations for choosing your location though, the most important ones being proximity of accommodation and provision of food. In your schedule, you'll need to consider which part of the location you'll be using while you're setting up in another area. Finally, there's the weather – something that you don't have to worry about in a studio. Make sure you have supplies to tackle wet, cold or hot weather situations, such as lots of umbrellas, towels, heat packs, jackets, ice packs and sunscreen. If you're in a period setting, you'll need to check that there are enough plug sockets for all the equipment. You'll still need to allocate spaces for a green room, costume changing and make-up. You will also need to work with the location owners or managers to make sure your filming won't damage any real antiques.

The last step in pre-production will be to hire a runner. You will definitely need one. Usually, the PM will have some recommendations, but if you or the director have someone in mind, make sure you pass on their CVs to the PM. It helps if the runner can drive, too. If they can drive a van, extra bonus points.

During the shoot, you will probably need to take on a role that is equivalent to an AD, an assistant director. Here's a breakdown of the responsibilities of the various ADs:

First AD

If we're talking in *Game of Thrones* terms, the first AD is the Hand of the King – with the director being the King. During filming, the director will usually be watching the monitor to check that the scene is being acted and shot to their preference. If they have any comments or changes, they will instruct the first AD as to those changes, and the AD will then speak to the actors, while the director will speak to the DoP. It's the first AD who calls 'action'. They will also be monitoring the shooting schedule and checking with the second and third ADs whether everything is ready to move on to shooting the next scene – e.g. is the set dressed? Are the actors ready? For more information about the life of a first AD, I'd refer you to Liz Gill's excellent book, *Running the Show*.

Second AD

The role of the second AD is most similar to that of a producer. Being a second AD involves organisation, coordination, communication, people skills and problem-solving skills. It essentially involves keeping track of the SAs and actors, making sure that everything behind the scenes, or, rather, behind the set, is running smoothly. You need to look out for kit, props, special effects or additional features, such as horses and carriages and jibs and cranes. You need to make sure each actor and SA arrives on time, gets through make-up and costume within their allocated slot, and is ready and waiting in the green room with plenty of time to spare before the first AD calls them to set. If there are any mix-ups or delayed SAs, it will be your responsibility to solve the problem so that it doesn't impact the shooting schedule.

Third AD

Where the first AD answers to the director, the third AD answers to the first. The Hand of the Hand of the King, essentially. Or perhaps a finger. Anyway, enough of this analogy, what it means in practical terms is that the third AD should be on set helping the first unless the first asks them to go and wrangle actors or SAs. The third is responsible for making sure the cast move between the costume and hair and make-up departments to schedule, then bringing them down to set. Once on set, the third is in charge of directing the background or SAs. This can result in a lot of creative authority, as the director would not usually direct the background (and if the director addresses an SA, this means you have to pay them more), so the third can position them wherever they like and instruct their movements. In drama reconstruction, you will likely be working with very few SAs, so this may not be relevant for productions you work on, but in larger drama productions, there can be tens or hundreds of background artists, which can make the third's job much more exciting!

Top tips

Things to look out for during the shoot:

- AWOL SAs. Unfortunately, sometimes the SAs are late or don't turn up. You may have to do some imaginative reshuffling of the schedule or the casting so that this doesn't interrupt or delay shooting. Whatever you do, make sure you communicate your plan clearly to the director or first AD. If you are at a loss for what to do, consult the director.

- Badly behaved directors. Shoots can be stressful, but there is no excuse for taking out that stress on a fellow crew member. If the director, or anyone else for that matter, behaves aggressively or inappropriately towards you, do not let it slide. Tell your PM and, if necessary, lodge a complaint with the production company. Silence perpetuates bullying and abuse: we are all responsible for speaking out and stopping it. Equally, if you realise you have spoken to someone inappropriately or harshly, apologise at the first opportunity you get.

- **Drama in costume/hair and make-up**. Lots of people in small rooms with hot tongs, steamers and clothes pins...it can be a petri dish for frayed tempers. Often it blows over quickly, but be prepared to resolve minor disagreements in a diplomatic way. Distance is usually a good solution – perhaps identify a nearby breakout room.

- **Female chaperones on set**. If there were more diversity within film (especially drama) crews, this wouldn't have to be a consideration for the drama producer. However, as it stands, there must be a female chaperone on set for any female actors or SAs participating in intimate scenes. The director is ultimately responsible for this, but you should keep an eye on it too.

- **Paperwork**. Stay on top of your release forms and the recorded hours for your SAs. It'll be very difficult to catch up on this after the shoot, so it's worth taking a few minutes throughout the day to make sure all your paperwork is completed.

- **Radios**. If you have someone across DIT at the end of the shoot, then they are responsible for the radios, but it's worth double-checking that everyone has returned their radios at the end of the day and that they are charging overnight.

This is not an exhaustive list: every shoot is different. You'll need your problem-solving mindset to hand at all times.

Final tip: go to bed. There is an after-work drinking culture, especially among drama crews, but remember that the most important thing is being ready for work the next day. If you don't want to stay late, make your excuses and go to bed. Although the crew's time is carefully measured, productions can try to take liberties with yours. Protect yourself and your reputation by making sure you get enough rest to be able to perform professionally for the whole shoot.

I was once on a shoot where I was obliged to turn up an hour before everyone else to prep radios, scripts and schedules – then, after a 12-hour shooting day, I had to organise dinner for the whole cast and crew. While they relaxed, ate curry and drank whisky, I was clearing plates and washing glasses until midnight, with a 5am start the following day. It was too much; I was exhausted and grumpy, when I normally pride myself on being chirpy and enthusiastic. It ruined what should have been a very exciting job. If you find yourself in a similar situation, speak to the PM. You may feel under pressure to go above and beyond every day, but it's not worth compromising your work just for the sake of appearances.

Branded content producer

There's a growing demand for traditional TV producers in corporate communications. TV producers have an advantage here over PR or advertising agencies, because we know how to tell a compelling, entertaining story that keeps people in their seats and leaves them wanting more. Another advantage to non-scripted producers making branded content is that our penchant for telling human stories through people's own words resonates powerfully with an audience that is now so used to being continuously sold to that they develop, in the words of Shane Smith, the Executive Chairman of Vice Media, a 'sophisticated bullsh*t detector'. The authentic, compelling approach of non-scripted content makes a brand seem more trustworthy and more ethical.

The basic principle of making corporate communications is the same as traditional television – you establish what the story is, you identify the audience, and then you structure that story to make it attractive and appropriate to the audience. But corporate productions tend to be a lot shorter than broadcast – 2–10 minutes maximum, rather than broadcasting slots of 30 minutes to 1 hour.

Another big difference is the communication challenge. In TV, we choose and pitch our own stories based on what we think will make the best programme. In the corporate world, the stories are already chosen for us – and our challenge lies in the way we tell that story. The second challenge lies in the workload – as a branded content producer, you are often the development, shooting, edit and post-producer all in one! It makes for a lot of responsibility but also a strong sense of ownership over the final product.

The process of making a branded content film begins with a meeting with the client. This could be a travel company, a large corporation or even a communications agency that is delegating the filmmaking aspect of their campaign to you. The client will brief you on their requirements: their rough idea of what they want it to be like, the objective they want to achieve through the film, and the target audience. If these are not clear from the client's brief, make sure you push to have those questions answered. Ask for style references, if possible.

Once they have sent you the brief, it's then your job to go away and think of ideas for how to make a good film. As a non-scripted filmmaker, this will likely involve finding contributors, or perhaps setting up a game format. Once you've worked up your idea, you'll then present it to the client. After a couple of rounds of feedback, your idea will be approved and you can start casting and setting up. You'll team up with a PM for this, plus you'll also likely need a lot of cooperation from the client to secure the contributors and outreach. With corporate clients, this process can take a lot longer than in traditional TV – normally, we would just contact the people we want in our film, or at least their agents, but with branded content there is often red tape to go through with the client and various data protection procedures. Scheduling your shooting dates will also depend a lot on the client, rather than your talent's availability.

If you self-shoot, you may film your own material, or alternatively you could hire a DoP and soundie team. You may even choose to hire an additional director for the shoot itself. It all depends on the budget, time constraints and scope of the film you've been asked to make, so each project will have its own set of rules. Once you've got your rushes ingested, you'll then settle down to edit – for more information on this, see the edit producer section on p.116. Like the pitch, the edit will go back and forth to the client for feedback – but try to keep this to two or three rounds, as for traditional television. For branded content, however, you will likely have to deal with feedback from far more stakeholders than in traditional television, and many of these stakeholders will have little to no idea about how to make a film. As such, it's wisest to send them a rough cut that's closer to a fine cut, as they will often end up criticising things at rough-cut stage that are obviously going to be changed – or rather, obvious to you that they're going to be changed. You will need to be patient with your client and carefully explain the production process to them from the very beginning: why you need all this kit, why you need this much time, why this storyline won't work etc. Once you become familiar with the techniques of storytelling, it's easy to forget that many people don't think in the same way and need to have these basic tenets explained to them. After all, you were once learning this stuff, too...

Once the film has been approved, your post-production process will not likely involve credits, but rather branded end plates and watermarks. However, you will still need to consider ASTONs and grading. Take a look at the edit producer section for more on this.

Development producer

The development producer role is a natural progression on from the development researcher role. You may reach this via a short stint as a development AP, but the responsibilities are much the same across the roles.

There are four main additional responsibilities that you'll have as a development producer compared to a development researcher. The first is a greater capacity to review work, the second is a developed ability to spot trends and good stories, the third is more consideration of the production aspects, while the fourth is more interaction with commissioners (although the execs will still take the lead on this).

1. **Review work**. As the development producer, you will now be reviewing the researcher's work and improving it. The key here is, quite simply, experience. Over the course of your career you will improve your writing skills (particularly if you deliberately set yourself the challenge of writing for different audiences) and understand what makes for a compelling pitch. Even if it seems difficult to imagine now, if you're just starting out, with time it will become obvious that one way of phrasing something is better than another, that a certain section is superfluous, that some sentences sound better merged or separated, or that there is a clearer way to communicate an idea. Sometimes this is as simple as casting a fresh pair of eyes on a piece of work, but sometimes (if you remember our section on researching), the person initially working up the project has got too far into the detail and needs someone to pull them back to the bigger picture. You will have that experience and that growing tingling sense of what makes a good story, so you can effectively adapt and improve a researcher's work.

2. **Spot stories and trends**. What makes for a good story? There are many formulae that try to encapsulate the key components of a strong story. Many of them are valid and useful, but every now and then along comes an incredible story that breaks all the rules. It reminds me of when I used to produce an improv comedy group – they would workshop various techniques and hone them until they were second-nature, but every now and then they sensed, in the course of a sketch, that it would actually be funnier to break those rules. I think this can be applied to TV storytelling, too. Make sure you learn the rules and shortcuts and tips and tricks for what makes a good story – but as you look for the Next Big Thing, make sure you keep an open mind. Don't be afraid to take risks if you feel that there is a strong story in spite of the odds. Equally, as you become more familiar with the tone of different broadcast or streaming channels and understand what makes for a successful story, you will be able to spot trends in broadcasting and capitalise on them, or identify a strong potential TV programme from a news story. Even if you're swamped with developing existing pitches and treatments, it's good to carve out an hour or so a week to scour for stories

and hone that story-sense. Keep a note of your ideas and pitch them at development brainstorming sessions.

3. **Production**. In Chapter 4, we briefly discussed how to think ahead and visualise how the show could work in production. As a development producer, this consideration becomes more important. You may even be doing some of the initial setting up of the show yourself, as you contact potential contributors or develop relationships with people in organisations or locations that you want to film. As you're making these setup calls, you will need to think like a development producer, story producer and producer director all at the same time. You'll be mentally checking the relevance of the story, location or contributor to your developed idea and the channel's scope; you'll be working out how this feeds into the overall story of the programme; and you'll be checking the practicalities of filming. This level of diligence ensures that you don't sell the commissioner a dud story that can't be followed through, and that you don't screw over the production team by bequeathing them a logistical nightmare.

4. **Commissioners**. The development executive at your production company will still handle direct relationships with commissioners and will still attend or look out for content calls, but if the exec is discussing the pitches or treatments you're working on, you will likely be involved in the meeting. Make sure you're prepared: you should be fully up to date with the latest version of your pitch or treatment and ideally have some extra information up your sleeve for the commissioner. If you're discussing an idea you've been working up for a while, take careful note of any feedback, suggestions or concerns the commissioner has. However, you may be meeting the commissioner to run some quick elevator pitches past them – again, be prepared, know the subject matter well, and be ready with extra information in case they are interested in an idea and want to know more. These qualities and tips will make you stand out in those meetings.

Some people find that they love development and specialise in this area of TV, but personally I find it quite creatively draining and need a little break occasionally. Doing a bit of production work in between development contracts also ensures that you stay up to date with the latest production techniques and realities, which means that when you start developing an idea, you have a better understanding of what is possible to achieve on the ground.

Edit producer

Get ready to make a new best friend. You will be spending eight or more hours a day with them, in one small, usually quite warm room, five days a week, for a month or more. This new best friend is your editor.

Together, you and your editor will craft the final film, the final product that the world will see. Everything that happened before is leading up to this moment, which, for me, is my favourite time in the production process.

Sync pull

Before you even get into the edit suite, you will need to do your sync pull. We already covered this briefly in the edit AP section on p. 90, but this section will go into the sync pull in more detail. The first step is to get hold of your timecoded transcripts (the PM should have sent off your interviews to be transcribed as soon as the rushes are returned) and read through them all once to refresh your memory. Some edit producers then like to set up a document, or series of documents, organised by topics that are relevant to the finished film, and then copy-paste interesting or useful bits of the transcript into these topic-based sections. I personally don't like that method, and instead I simply go through all the transcripts and highlight the bits I think are good and could be used in the film. Remember, at this early stage, you are casting the net very wide indeed – just pick out sections that are really good. You will refine them later.

Once you have this complete overview of all your material, then you can move on to constructing the edit script.

Edit script

You should have a shooting script to hand, either one that you have written yourself or one that has been bequeathed to you by the director. Now, I knew of one edit producer who never looked at the shooting script and simply

Table 6.1 How to format sync in an edit script

VISUAL	AUDIO
James Holland IV **Clip HOLLAND_070222_A001**	10:05:20 The invasion of Sicily was a triumph, ~~er, despite the extreme weather conditions that plagued the air and sea forces and, and, and probably caused more casualties than were strictly necessary, er, but for the commanders they had to balance that out against the benefit of the element of surprise, um, because~~ thanks to the success of Operation Mincemeat, the German forces on Sicily had been moved elsewhere, leaving it vulnerable to Allied attack

reconstructed the film from scratch according to the available material – he was an established maverick, however, and it's better to start with some sort of structure, even if you end up changing most of it. Go through the shooting script to check what sync the director intended to capture (known as 'wish sync') and see how well it matches up with the material in your transcripts. In all likelihood, your transcripts will contain gems that get to the story point much better than the wish sync, or even add a new dimension to the story. Save a new copy of the shooting script as the first draft of your edit script and start populating it with the sync that fits the story. Table 6.1 gives an example of how to format your fresh sync.

The clip name in the VISUAL section tells your editor where to find the visuals, while the numbers in the AUDIO section identify which timecode to search for in the footage to find this piece of sync. Highlight new sync to be inserted, then un-highlight it once the editor has put it in place. Cross out any parts of their sync that need to be cut.

Start a new row for every clip, every piece of archive, every piece of comm or VO, and every sequence. Basically, if someone new starts speaking, start a new row.

However, you may find that you are missing some sections of the story-line – either because they simply weren't filmed or the story evolved during filming. You will have to see where else the story takes you in the material you have and rewrite those sections.

If the film is presenter-led, you will also need to add in clips and timecodes of relevant pieces to camera, if you have the transcripts; but if not, simply put in the day that piece of material was filmed, if known.

You'll usually have about a week to construct your edit script – once you've established the bare bones of your sync, you're ready to go into the edit and meet your new best friend.

> Golden Rule: don't keep editing the same edit script document – always save off new copies after each major revision. You may subsequently want to go back to a previous version to find a bit of sync you cut but now want to reinsert, or revert back to a previous structure.

Getting into the edit

Prior to starting the edit, the technician in the post-house or production company should have uploaded all your footage to 'bins' within the editing software. Hopefully, they will have labelled them in a sensible manner – usually according to the labels given to the footage by whoever was covering the DIT on the shoot. Footage that's relevant to your episode should therefore be in the correct bin. The first task for the editor is to look through all the footage in the bins to see what they can work with.

If you have already directed the material you're about to edit, you're at an advantage. You'll know what the rushes are, you'll know how you want to cut them into your script, and you can start working on it straight away with your editor. The first thing to do is pull out all the sync into a sequence, then while you review the quality of the sync and write/record the comm, your editor can start filling in the gaps with visuals. You will also record any VO as you go – yes, that means you, your voice, recording the placeholder VO on your film. Many people dislike the sound of their own voice – unfortunately, if this applies to you, you may have to get over it! Or get the editor to record the VO if they have a better reading voice. Remember, when you are recording the VO, speak slowly and clearly to mimic the way a real voiceover artist would do it. Timing is important, especially when you get further down the line with your film.

If you weren't the director but have come in as a standalone edit producer, then you should embark on a similar process. You'll have already prepared your edit script based on the materials provided, and ideally you should have had the opportunity to look through the rushes yourself too. Then it's the same process: pull your sync and fill in the gaps.

Rough cut

For an hour-long documentary, the rough cut should take between two and three weeks to craft. Of course, you will get less time for shorter films. The rough cut is a constant iterative process: you pull your sync, put it all together, add visuals (archive, GVs or sequences), go back through, refine everything (usually cutting it right down), then rethink the visuals, smooth the transitions and add the music. Sometimes the editor likes to add music during the process, sometimes they'll prefer to do it towards the end of the rough cut so they don't have to keep recutting the music as you tweak the visuals. Your rough cut should not be significantly longer than the length of the final film, although it definitely shouldn't be shorter.

At the end of the rough-cut process, you will send the film to be viewed by the SP, sometimes the exec as well. They are not expecting perfection, but they are expecting a solid storyline containing all the key elements (bar features like graphics, which may be in the process of being constructed). Ideally, this viewing should happen in person, but in the post-Covid world it is sometimes easier to do this remotely and for the SP to give notes afterwards. These may be in the form of an email with timecodes or as comments inserted directly on the timecodes of the film – depending on what viewing software is being used.

When you receive your feedback, even if it feels harsh, try not to be that person who can't take criticism. The SP is usually more experienced and their feedback is generally constructive, even if it feels like they're tearing your film apart. If there is a comment you fundamentally disagree with, have a discussion about it with your SP and explain the reasons behind your creative choice. Together you should be able to work out a solution.

Fine cut

Now it's time to act on those changes recommended by the SP, as well as any further adjustments you've thought of as a result of your rough-cut viewing. Make sure you're keeping your edit script fully up to date with your changes. As the sync you've pulled goes into the film, you will need to un-highlight it and delete any crossed-out sections, so that the script is simply a faithful transcript of the contents of the film itself. Make sure also to update the VISUAL column with a brief description of the scene, interviewee, archive or visuals. Again, you can remove the clip names and numbers as they are inserted into the film. At this stage, your editor will also be making 'invisible edits', little changes they can see in the timeline that will make the film look much smoother but won't have a structural impact. It's a gradual process of polishing and refining.

Your fine cut will be viewed by your SP, the exec and the commissioner. Together with the link to your film, you will need to submit a timecoded edit script. For this, you will need to add an extra column to your script headed TIMECODE and add the timecode at the beginning of each row. You may be able to ask an AP or researcher to do this for you, depending on the staffing level of the production at this stage. As an AP, I once returned home at 11pm after a late dinner with a friend to timecode a fine-cut script the edit team had only just finished...but we managed to submit all the materials just before the 'end of day' deadline the commissioner had set!

Picture-lock

After your fine-cut viewing, you should only have relatively minor changes to make. Typically, there is only a week between fine cut and picture-lock, so any major structural changes should either have been caught earlier or result in an extension of the edit. This is also the stage where you will insert any graphics that have been made for your film and really polish your VO or commentary. Once your film has picture-locked, then you'll have a session in a recording studio with your voiceover artist or presenter to record the VO lines.

There will be one more viewing to confirm picture-lock, then your work is done! At this stage, you will probably say goodbye to your editor and your contract. If you are kept on, however, the next stage is to go into grading, credits and captions.

Grading, credits and captions

In your edit script, you will have included (in the VISUAL column) the appropriate captions for any contributor who appears in your film. These captions are also called ASTONs or CHYRONs. For example: Professor

R. R. R. Smith, Oxford University, or June Sawkins, Accountant. You (or the researcher on the project) will need to double-check with your contributors the appropriate captions for their appearance in the film. These are then inserted into the final film according to the style determined by the executive or SP for the series or programme. This is done by a post-production specialist, who will also develop the credits list. This is usually put together by the PM, but if you are around at this stage in the production, you may be asked to check names. The film will also be professionally graded.

Once this final film has been checked, checked again and checked a final time, it will be sent off to the commissioner. Congratulations, you finished a film! Now all you have to do is wait until it broadcasts (known in telly terms as the TX date).

Summary

- As a producer, the whole production is in your head. Stay on top of your emails and conversations.
- Building relationships is a crucial skill in this role
- Producing can be a very varied remit – enjoy the range of jobs or start to specialise

What to watch

- Content your industry friends have made
- Short films from up-and-coming directors (attend Sheffield DocFest)
- Content you wish you had made

Chapter 7

Director

This is the top of the editorial ladder, the perfect balance of creative engagement, editorial control and overall vision. Any further up the ladder, to series producer (SP) or executive producer (EP), and you lose tactile contact with the finished film: you have oversight of it, but you are not involved with the day-to-day making of the film on the ground.

Stepping up

Like the step up from assistant producer (AP) to producer, your best bet for advancing from producer or AP to director is within a company that you know well, with whom you have worked many times before. It is also more common in smaller production companies. When you feel ready to step up, you will need to speak to everyone with whom you have a good relationship in that production company: other directors, heads of production, production managers (PMs), series producers. Once you have made it clear that you are looking for a directing role, then you must also insist that you will not take another job at the production company unless it is a directing job. Be firm about this: at this point in your career, you will be very well networked, highly regarded as an AP or producer and greatly in demand from other production companies. The worst that can happen is that you get another producing role. Hold out for your step up and make clear your worth. It doesn't matter what kind of production you work on that gets you the directing credit: it just matters that you get it. As soon as you have one, you will be able to get others far more easily.

The first section of this chapter will cover the three different types of directors in TV: DV directors, producer directors (PDs) (by far the most common) and shooting PDs.

The second section of this chapter will focus on the five key elements of directing Factual TV: scripting, interviews, actuality, drama reconstruction and presenters.

DOI: 10.4324/9781003294009-8

DV director: interview with Alec Lindsell

The DV director can be an intermediary role between shooting AP and shooting PD. It's ideal if you enjoy shooting, and you're good at it, but need to develop your editorial skills more. A DV director will shoot sequences that are supplementary to the main action, like GVs (general views), non-sync (non-speaking) sequences or even second storylines. You will need to have a strong understanding of the requirements of the script, plus your own creative input in terms of how best to tell the supplementary story elements through the shots you choose. You'll also need to think ahead to the edit – imagine how those shots are going to be used when it comes to the editing suite. Let's hear more detail on DV directing from Alec Lindsell:

> Since I was never actually a shooting AP, my move from being a camera operator/editor to being a director/DV director wasn't the conventional one, so isn't necessarily relevant to people who go through the ranks of runner/researcher/AP/director etc. But ultimately, because I was technically minded and worked as a camera op and editor in tandem, I was eventually tasked with roles that saw me DV directing.
>
> Being a DV director often means you're filming things like GVs or pickups or additional shots, which the main director won't be able to get. You may also be required to shoot as a second camera on an interview between a contributor and a presenter (shooting researchers/ shooting APs also do this), but mostly you'll be asked to go off alone and film elements away from the crew. On these occasions, the SP or PD will have briefed you on what they want, whether it's a list of GVs or shots you must get, or, if conducting an interview, what to ask the contributor. Ultimately, a DV director is a bit like the second unit director in a film. You'll be getting things which will require some creative input, but which do not form the main structure of the final project.
>
> HOW TO BE THE BEST DV DIRECTOR:
>
> 1. **Be specific to the show**. Stylistically, you should have a good idea of how the show shoots. There's no point in you going off and shooting a load of GVs in a heavily stylised manner if the show is straight-edged. And conversely, if the show has a particular style to it and your DV director input doesn't reflect this, then the shots will stand out and may not be useable, so a conversation with the director and/or DoP about what they want from these shots is crucial.
>
> 2. **Knowing your camera is vital**. So often people get into technical positions via editorial roles – a researcher who is asked to shoot, for example, will get sent on a two- or three-day course; however, a few days won't do the job. It takes a while to learn to

shoot well – it's not just the technical aspects of how to operate a camera but also framing, exposure, focus, lenses etc., which are not really covered in depth on these short courses. While a DV director isn't required to shoot as well as a shooting PD or DoP, they *will* need to be competent and capable of obtaining the necessary shots required for the project, and you'll likely have to do it in double-quick time too. Therefore, one of the best things anyone aspiring to being a DV director and then a shooting PD can do is practise and become familiar with all aspects of shooting. This will not only make you better at the job but help accelerate the transition between roles. Study shows on TV, work out where the camera is positioned, look at the shots the edit is using when it comes to GVs and cutaways. What framing is being used, what camera moves are being used? This means that you not only need to have an idea about what type of shots you're expected to get but also where those shots may fit in in the final edit.

3. **Learn some stock shots**. Because time is always a factor, you'll have to think fast and work fast. As you continue to work, you'll build up a catalogue in your brain (you can also note them down on paper) of stock shots, which you can apply to various types of show and/or subject. Let's say you have to get some GVs of a stately home for a show, you'll likely want a wide shot, and to pick out four or five close-up details: windows, chimney pots, ornate styling. Then you may also pick up a tilt-down to reveal the building. These are shots that could be applied to a council house or a government building, depending on the show you're working on. The same can be said of shooting most other GVs. Whether it's a pan across, a tilt-down to reveal or a focus pull, you'll know these basic shots, which work, so you can get the job done quickly. *Location, Location, Location* or *A Place in the Sun* are great shows to watch to get an idea of these very stock shots – you'll see the same formula repeated across the programme's several houses.

4. **Be efficient/Plan ahead**. To go along with the above tip, it will also help if you plan which shots you're going to get before you put your camera in place. Is there a position where you can knock out several shots without having to reposition (even with a change of lens)? That doesn't mean you should be lazy about getting the right things. You should always aim to get the best-quality shot and what the show requires, but equally, work smart. If you can get those things from three positions instead of six positions, then it would make sense, both in time and for your body as you move

the kit around. If you're directing a person who is performing an action, then work out what you may need and discuss it with the subject first. Keeping them in the loop will help them stay on side (as we all know, not everyone understands that a lot of filming is repeating things and often takes far longer than the average person on the street anticipates). These discussions can open up new avenues for you when directing. Let's say you're filming a scientist in a lab performing a basic experiment – I would ask them to talk/walk me through exactly what they're going to do first. As they do this I will be thinking/plotting/jotting down the shots we'll pick up:

a. A wide of them performing the whole thing
b. Close-ups on the test tubes
c. Then on to the machine they're using etc.

In working out the process and the shots, you may be told about something else they can do which looks more impressive or an angle which is more camera friendly, or that they can do it again for you later so you can get a better shot. Along with that you may discover that the process is a one-hit deal which cannot be repeated, so you need to make sure you capture it in one go and are not changing shot or repositioning yourself right when the key moment is happening. This on-the-spot planning is vital to being an efficient DV director and, subsequently, a shooting PD.

Producer director

This is the most common type of directing role in Factual TV. It combines all the logistical skills you will have learned as an AP or producer with the creative oversight of the film: including how it looks. By this point in your career, you will be expected to know about cameras, even if you've never used one yourself. You will need to know the different types of shots, how to blend them together in order to create a story through pictures, rather than just words, as well as the different types of cameras and their relative advantages and disadvantages, plus lens types and sizes. Some of this you will learn simply through watching others do it – that said, I would highly recommend that you attend a camera course at some point in your career in order to learn about these things. Ask lots of questions on your course too, to get the most out of it. Screenskills offers many camera courses for people at all different levels, plus some production companies proactively fund courses. Remember, you're shooting for the edit, thinking with the finished film in mind and working backwards to determine what material you need to shoot in order to get that film looking the way you want it. Therefore, it helps to have some edit experience before you become a PD – although, as I mentioned on p. 100, often people need to become a PD before they become an edit producer. A flaw in the system, you might say. You can get round this by making your own films in your spare time and editing them yourself, or alongside an editor, in order to learn how the process works. By the time I became a director, I had edited two of my own films, as well as spending eight months as an edit AP, so I was very familiar with what it takes to shoot for the edit.

We will cover the different shot types you'll need to think about later, but first, let's tackle what happens when you first start a project as a PD. Either you'll be the first on the project, or you'll come on a couple of weeks after the rest of the team (depending on how the PM has decided to manage budgeting and scheduling for the project). If you're the first person on there, your primary task will be to familiarise yourself with the commissioned treatment and any available beat sheets. You'll then need to do a deep dive into the subject matter: identifying the key plot points in the storyline, what extra research is needed, which points are unclear, what needs fact checking. Draw up a research list that you can then pass on to your AP or researcher to tackle, while you work on getting a thorough overview. Draw up a book list, order books if you need them, read articles, check websites, speak to anyone you know who has covered similar subject matter. Then, once the rest of the team joins you, you'll be in a good place to delegate work. If it's a format or game show or even a recurring series, familiarise yourself with previous episodes. If it's a new format, speak to the development team about the concept they pitched to the commissioner.

If you join the production later, the first thing you'll need to do is talk to the key members of the team. Book in a chat with the SP to get an overview of the programme and how it fits with any other episodes. Speak to the PM to get an understanding of the budget allocations for locations, contributors, travel, shooting period and any other important details. Then get together with your AP and researcher to find out what they've already covered. Ask them to brief you on their impression of the story and key research points. You'll then need to catch up with their research and direct their work according to your vision of the story. Finally, speak to any other directors on the project, to see what their experience and impressions have been.

Ideally, you'll want a few weeks of research time before you begin to think about scripting – although this depends on the schedule. Once you feel as though you are on top of the research and have internalised that information, you will need to start shaping it into a script. We've already covered a lot of the scripting process in our AP and producer sections – for more details on the scripting process, please head to p. 136.

As you develop the shooting script, you'll also need to be across choosing, scheduling and interviewing your contributors. Much of the basic scheduling you should be able to delegate to your AP, but you will also need to oversee this process, adding input where necessary. You (perhaps together with your AP) will also write the interview questions for the contributors. Have a look at p. 139 for more information on how to prepare the interview questions and direct the interviews.

Depending on the type of Factual TV you're making, you may also need to source archive or film actuality, drama reconstruction or presenter-led sequences. As you write your script, you should add as much detail as possible to the VISUAL column – what you see in your head as the words in the AUDIO section are heard. Sometimes, though, this structure squashes visual creativity– go back through your script and check if any of what you've written in the AUDIO section can be communicated with a visual sequence only. As you prepare for your shoot, go through your script and pull out what you need for a shot list. It can be helpful to then break down that shot list per each shooting location. As an AP, you should already have perfected the daily folder method – don't lose sight of this just because you are now an important director! Remember, the more thinking you do in advance of the shoot, the easier it will go for you and the fewer problems you'll have to solve on the ground when you're short of time, potentially hot and thirsty, or cold and hungry, and managing a whole crew. Prepare your daily folders with your own copies of the call sheet, script, shot lists and interview questions, if you're doing interviews on location.

As you prepare these editorial responsibilities, you'll also need to keep an eye on the preparations happening on production's side. Try to avoid being overbearing and micromanaging; instead aim to be helpful and offer your broader experience. Check in daily or every couple of days with your AP just to go over what they've been working on, allocate them further tasks and cross-reference with your to-do list. Be sure to go over the shooting schedule in great detail with them: you need to double-check that enough time has been allocated for each sequence and location. Some directors work more efficiently than others, but at the same time it also takes someone with plenty of experience to know how much time certain sequences take, depending on the weather, the terrain, the subject matter, the contributor or the presenter.

While you're thinking about all this, you will also need to speak to the PM about booking crew. Most directors have a preferred camera operator or DoP with whom they like to work. If you have a favourite, check their availability as soon as you know your shooting dates, as they will get booked up quickly. That said, try to be open to new people: TV is a nepotistic industry based on networks, which can be a benefit when you have a good working relationship with someone and know that you will collaborate efficiently together, but can also result in the ranks of the 'old boy' network closing in against new talent. If you are open to working with new people, you may just find your next favourite person. If your PM gives you the option of a soundie too, always take it. It makes a world of difference having the sound professionally recorded. If your PM has not already considered this, make an effort to check the diversity of the crew. I have lost count of the number of times I have recommended female crew members or people of colour only to have both the PM and the director close ranks and choose white men. Unless the contributor or presenter is female, I have also often been the only woman on the crew. It gets very boring, and it's not for a lack of talented women. The responsibility for this lies with you: although the PM has a lot of power, you, as the director, have more sway when it comes to editorial decisions.

The final thing to consider before you go on shoot is what kit you want. Your DoP will probably bring their own kit, but you will need to consult them about the most suitable camera to bring, as they may have multiple options. The quality of camera you can afford will depend on the production's budget, but you'll also have to take into account whether extra lenses will need to be hired and whether they are compatible with the DoP's camera – if they are not, but you still want the lenses, you'll also need to hire an adaptor. Remember that if you're shooting inside, you'll also need to bring lighting. Your production company should provide you with stock, the industry term for cards (e.g. SD, CF, SxS, XQD). Check with your DoP what cards their camera takes, and make sure the production company gives you plenty of that type. You should allow for three cards per day, plus two spare. The AP or DoP will usually back up the cards every evening to two hard drives – one master and one backup – so you'll be able to reuse them the next day. Remember to split the master and backup drives between you and your AP – so if one of you loses your bag or it gets stolen, at least you have another one in a different place.

Shooting PD Alec Lindsell has put together the following very basic kit list. You can embellish this with extra equipment or upgrade the kit according to budget. Remember that the standard TV camera changes every few years, so be sure to stay up to date with the latest developments.

Basic kit list

- Sony FS7mk I or mk II/Sony FX9/Canon C300
- A good shoulder rig
- For the FS7/FX9 – a Shape Quick Release Arm (you will want this if filming on the shoulder)
- For the FS7/FX9 – XDCA V-lock extension. This allows for V-lock batteries to be used, which last longer, and also will give the camera a better balance on the shoulder as well as allow for timecode synching with other cameras/sound operator.

- V-lock batteries
- 24–105mm lens
- 70–200mm lens
- 50mm prime lens
- (Occasionally a 16mm–35mm lens)
- A good tripod. A Sachtler tripod is recommended – one with single-locking legs for speed and ease of use. Often supplied are DV12/Video 18/20 or the newer Aktiv 8/10. These tripods are not too heavy, so they can be easily carried around.
- If you are having to record your own sound, then a pair of Sennheiser G3 radio mics or Sony UWP-D27/K33 dual channel kit is recommended
- Sennheiser ME66 or MKH416 shotgun mic to work either as a top mic for the camera or a boom mic on a pole with a long XLR cable
- A good set of headphones like the sennheiser hd 25 light or sony mdr-7506/1
- Two or three Bi-Colour LED light panels and lightweight stands with V-lock batteries and mains power adaptors

This kit is suitable for a multitude of styles and types of shoot – you can use this for actuality, on-the-shoulder, obs-doc, sit-down interviews, presenter-led content. It's a versatile kit that can be taken around by one or ideally two people.

Don't forget the following extras, provided by the production company:

- Stock (cards)
- Electric tape and Sharpie (to label the cards)
- Two hard drives
- Card readers

After the shoot, you will either move on to edit your own film or hand over to the edit producer. If you get the opportunity, try to sit down with the edit producer and brief them on anything that changed during the shoot, any elements of the script that you weren't able to shoot or were modified, and what story points are the most important to hit. If you do not get this opportunity, write a handover note or keep notes during the shoot that you can then pass on. Better still, annotate the rushes log with these notes. After that – trust the edit producer. It can be hard when you've been so invested in your project, but remember that they too are experienced professionals and will make the best film they can.

Shooting PD

A shooting PD has to do all of the above – and operate the camera! Sometimes even handle sound as well. It's definitely a lot to think about, but on the plus side, you are fully in control of not only the editorial structure but also the content.

We'll now hear some advice from a few shooting PDs:

Interview with Sophie Smith

It's hard to pinpoint exactly how to get your first shooting PD gig, everyone's route through their television career and story is different. There is no single way. Stay focused and believe in your ability.

When I started in television a DV director wasn't really a thing; now it's become an additional stepping stone in most genres to becoming a self-shooting PD. I believe this has come about as budgets have tightened and lot of companies are able to exploit aspiring self-shooting PDs into becoming DV directors on the premise it's 'good experience' rather than a much cheaper way of employing someone to do the same job. Anyway, that's the way it seems to be now and I can't see it changing. For me, it was via DV director that I landed my first shooting PD role – I had done a contract as a DV director and then a separate project urgently needed a shooting PD. I agreed to do it and negotiated a shooting PD credit. Basically, right place, right time. Once you gain your first credit, you then have to be selective about your next roles. Don't be afraid to say no. This can be really hard as many jobs want additional experience, so speaking to companies and people you know is hugely beneficial at this stage.

Every project is different but ultimately, as the PD, you are responsible for the team around you and the end product. Having a clear vision of what you're working towards is vital and communicating this with your team to ensure it happens is even more important. Support is a two-way necessity – you need to support and manage your team properly so they can support you in creating the programme you're trying to make. Communication is key. A PD on set is also responsible for the health and safety of their team and has to consider all variables with each role in a risk assessment to mitigate any risks. This includes mental as well as physical. Topics and environments vary hugely and some can be extremely challenging. As well as the welfare of your crew, a PD must always consider the welfare of their contributors. This is imperative not only for the contributors' welfare but also to ensure they feel relaxed, confident and clear about what will be asked of them to ensure the best content is captured during filming. With questions, work backwards from the answer you want. It depends on what type of programme you're making, but if you're looking for something more emotive, it's more about asking contributors how they felt as opposed to what happened. Anything factual can easily be covered in voiceover; the content you're getting from your contributors is about engaging the audience. Don't be afraid to go a bit off-piste too if something more comes out in the interview. Make sure it's relevant to your content though, or you'll have a lot of extra footage to trawl through in the edit.

There is a lot to think about and concentrate on when filming – including crew, contributors, location, kit, and it can be draining. You need to remain focused and prioritise if something unplanned occurs (which happens regularly!). Set as much as you can up beforehand, especially with your camera – check all the settings and test kit the day before to give yourself enough contingency time to deal with any issues. It's often the very small things that can have a huge knock-on effect and is not worth the risk of winging it on the day. Always check your sound. Without sound or even bad sound, you have no interview…

Don't be over-ambitious; there is no harm in striving to be the best researcher or AP that you can. It's not only important for learning the key skills but for managing your team more effectively – you will be a much stronger PD for it.

Interview with Alec Lindsell

Being a shooting PD is a big step up from DV directing. Not only are you shouldering most of the responsibility of a shoot, but you oversee other members of the team, and it is necessary to keep everyone in the loop as to what you need and how you're going to get it. You also must become proficient at several jobs all at once and balance those jobs effectively.

Your job breaks down into three main roles, which you sometimes undertake individually or all at once.

Producer: You liaise with the SP and EP to work out the content of the show. You may have a framework from the SP and EP but it may well be up to you to finalise the details or develop features from the broad brushstrokes of the brief. Ultimately, you're working out the story or content, finding contributors, approving archive and writing scripts either for shooting or for voiceover.

Director: This is the part where you direct the action, how interviews are conducted and what they look like, how actuality is recorded and plays out, and overseeing any other cameras you have on that action.

Camera op (the shooting part of shooting PD): Acting in the capacity of camera operator, you're often the main camera op but sometimes you operate a B-Cam while a DoP or camera operator takes charge of A-Cam. For this you need to be able to shoot to a high level, light for interviews and be adept at switching between different styles of filming, from obs-doc to actuality to sit-down interviews.

The additional jobs: More often than not, those three jobs aren't the only roles that shooting PDs are being asked to undertake. These days, due to budget constraints, shooting PDs are asked to record and monitor sound directly into the camera. They also have to act as their own researchers and, if being sent to shoots alone, take on some duties that would be dealt with by runners. A self-shooting PD needs to function either as part of a team or as a one-man/woman band.

1. How to direct sequences or capture what's happening in front of you effectively

Directing interviews is more about being a good interviewer than being a good director of action. You need to be across the story fully, build a good rapport with your subject/contributor and know how to ask open questions which allow them to tell their story effectively. You'll also need to assess when to ask key/crucial/difficult questions. Concise and confident questions are the way to go as they will clear up any vagueness and will give your contributor confidence that you are in control and are there to help them tell their story, not to trip them up or make them look stupid.

When it comes to directing actuality, the trick is to not get involved too much. You have to let what is about to happen play out. If you have too much input, then it stops being reality and starts to be something that has been produced and directed. One of the keys to this is to have the best possible knowledge of what is about to happen – this means discussing with the principal characters, or at least someone who knows the situation, what we're going to be seeing and filming. Is it someone arriving for a surprise reveal? Is it a hospital sequence where an operation is about to be performed? Is someone about to receive some news, either good or bad?

As far as possible you must work out the blocking. Where are people going to be standing and where is it best to put cameras? Are you going to be in the room with them and what will be the principal shot? If it's single camera, then you have to be aware of capturing the actuality and maybe coming back for pickups. You can delegate to a runner or researcher the task of noting down what is spoken about and where GVs will be needed.

If you have a B-Cam, then you need to establish what that camera will be getting. It could be on a safety wide shot to cover your movements, or covering one character while you cover another. Either way you have to have trust in your second shooter.

Knowing when to step in, ask questions or ask for something to be done again during actuality is a skill in itself. Mainly, you will need to know what the edit requires to tell that story, so it's not just a case of sticking your camera on the action, getting that and nothing else. Waiting for the right moment to ask your subject to answer a question is key; you don't want to take them out of a situation too soon or break their emotional direction, but at the same time you also want to know what is on their mind if they are not being forthcoming. Pick your moments carefully and be concise with your questions. The same goes for asking someone to repeat something, usually an action, but sometimes it can be words if they're key to the narrative and you were not able to get them the first time round. You don't want anyone to appear unnatural and you're not working with professional actors or presenters, so only ask for this if it's vital.

If what you're capturing is actuality but is being completed with knowledge of filming, then you have a bit more scope to get involved, ask for repeats and direct a little more, but the moment you interfere with actuality, then it stops being actual and starts becoming artificial. Less is more.

As a shooting PD you will have too many things to do and so you have to rely on your colleagues. A good sound operator is key and you should listen to the questions they may ask you about narrative as they will hear everything. If something isn't making sense to them, then it likely won't make sense to your audience. There have been times when a soundie has said to me that they didn't understand what was going on and it's only then you realise that an important bit of information has been missed, so you have time to pick it up.

2. Inside the mind of a shooting PD

You have to concentrate on your camera shot:

- Are you in focus?
- Is your friend OK?
- Is the sound going well?
- Is the exposure right?

Then you have to concentrate on the content:

- What are people saying?
- Are they saying what you need them to?
- Do you have to pick something up?
- But they made a mistake
- Is this the right time to ask them to repeat?

Then you have to focus on what your colleagues are doing:

- Are they filming the things I need them to get?
- Are they shooting B-Cam OK?
- Can I trust them?

You have to be thinking about all of these things at once! It's quite a pressurised situation and it's almost like running on a hamster wheel. But the best thing you can do is to know your camera extremely well. If you're struggling with the basics of shooting while also trying to control the content and direct the scene, and also concentrate on what your colleague or colleagues may be doing, then it's probably too many plates to spin and you're headed for a mistake.

3. What key skills you need to be a good shooting PD

The ability to multi-task. Being a self-shooting PD is all about multi-tasking. As a multi-skilled operator, you're performing at least three jobs at once so being able to balance the needs of each job is vital. You will have many plates spinning and you must shift seamlessly from wearing one hat to another.

Excellent people skills. You must be able to deal with people from all walks of life. One minute you'll be chatting with a single mum on a council estate, and the next could be the head of a major corporation, a member of the aristocracy or a homeless person on the street. Whatever the case, your role is to get them to tell you their story or answer your questions. Not only that but you'll be negotiating with people who won't be on camera, such as owners of venues, family or friends of contributors or agents. Being personable and being able to speak with everyone on their level in a clear and friendly way is vital.

Be a strong shooter. There are so many things going on all at once when you're working as a shooting PD that you rarely have time to think, so therefore being unsure about how to get the best out of your camera is something you just won't have room for. The basics of shooting should come naturally to you so that your attention is not consumed by these things when you are listening to a contributor.

Confidence. It's no surprise that as a shooting PD you need to exude confidence (not to be confused with arrogance). Walking into a room, onto a set or a location and being able to know what you want and demonstrate that to your team, your contributor and/or their people is key in being able to do your job well. Uncertainty from the person in charge will just lead people to be unsure of you and your abilities and that could lead to much worse things, such as other people trying to take over, step in and cause confusion etc. There's no shame in asking people questions, working through problems, positions, how actions will run etc., but these must all be done with confidence and then, following those discussions, a plan must be reached.

Patience. I've seen and heard directors get impatient with their contributors and crew before, and I can say this with confidence, that they did not get the best out of their subject or shoot. Not everyone is a natural in front of camera and surprisingly some presenters have their off-days too. Be patient with your contributors and your presenters. You are there to get the job done correctly, not rush through it so you can go home. If things aren't working out, then try a different approach, but shouting, screaming and getting outwardly annoyed will not help you or your crew or your shoot.

4. Tips and tricks for being the best shooting PD

Be organised. Being a self-shooting PD requires that you are organised in your approach to things. Yes, it's true that on a shoot things can go awry and you have to adapt and think on your feet, but the more organised you are to begin with, the more likely it is that you will have solutions to issues ready to go or have laid enough groundwork to find them. If things go well, then your organisation will pay off with a smooth shoot.

Check your script. We all usually write a script and/or plan for the day of shooting but you'd be surprised how many directors don't bother to check it once the cameras roll. Remind yourself or ask your AP/researcher/runner to remind you to check your script at regular intervals. You'd be surprised what you'll miss if you don't consult what you have pre-planned.

Have a think and a drink. Sometimes things just aren't working and you're not sure why or how to solve it. Even when you're up against it time-wise, the worst thing you can do is blindly carry on. The best course of action is to take 5 or 10 minutes out, grab a drink and think through the situation. A moment of calm or quiet can release the tension and answers will present themselves to you. This method has saved the day for many a director.

Don't be afraid to ask for what you want. Directing of any kind is telling people what to do so you can get what you need. I say telling, but this doesn't have be ordering people around, simply conveying clearly what you require. You can't expect the subject of your shoot to instinctively know what you're going to need and do it; you must ask them or brief them beforehand. But also, if you need someone to do something again, then ask them. Talk them through it clearly, demonstrate if you need to. This is also a good lesson to get the best out of your shoot. A contributor mentions an amazing artefact they have, a process you didn't know about or a place you know would be great to see for the project. Ask them if you can see it or go there. They may say no but, above all, if you don't ask you won't get. I've had people turn down my requests initially, either for access or a line of questioning or even their time, but once they get to know you or know the project, they can change their mind and suddenly you're getting that vital bit of information or going to the place which no one is normally allowed to see.

Work on your questioning technique. When it comes to asking questions, phrases like 'Tell me how', 'Talk me through' or 'Explain to me…' are great ways to make your questioning open. When getting the right kind of answers avoid phrases like 'Please can you put the question in the answer' as this often means your contributor will do something like say, 'How did I feel about that? Well, I felt this way…' and so on. I personally have always preferred to say, 'Could you answer in a full sentence – so if I asked you what you had for breakfast this morning, you wouldn't just say "cornflakes" you would say, "This morning for breakfast, I had cornflakes."' It gives the contributor an idea of how to answer a question in a way that works for the edit.

Be polite. I can't stress how important this is. Working as a shooting PD means dealing with people and getting them to do what you need them to do. If you're rude, they won't do it. If you're polite, friendly, nice, calm and respectful, even if your contributor is not, then you will get the best out of them. You'll get the best out of your crew and the shoot is much more likely to go well, or if it's not going well, your politeness will mean everyone is onside to help things move on.

You have to have great skills as an organiser, a people person, a technician and a scholar to be a great shooting PD. After all, you're doing the jobs of at least three people.

This wraps up the three different types of directors. We'll now move on to describe in more detail the skills you'll need to be an excellent director.

Scripting

We've covered several early development stages of scripts, such as storylines, beat sheets and sizzles. The final script for a programme is simply a longer evolution of this, which involves more detailed storytelling and more elements to balance.

As a general rule, one page of script equals one minute of screen time. So your script should be the same number of pages as the number of minutes in your programme.

The hardest part of scriptwriting is starting. It can feel very daunting to have just a blank page with your two VISUAL and AUDIO columns at the top and an intimidating number of rows below them. If you already have a beat sheet, I would recommend inserting elements of that into your script just to give yourself a starting point and remind yourself of the overall structure. Then close your eyes and watch the film playing out in your head. What's a captivating way for it to start? How can you grab the audience's attention right at the beginning? Where will you start the story? Where does it go next?

You have a number of building blocks with which to construct your script. These are:

- VO or comm
- Contributors/interviews
- Presenter pieces to camera (PTCs)
- Visual sequences
- Graphics
- Archive

Your show may not have all of these – e.g. there may not be a presenter, or no archive. Delete as appropriate and shuffle your building blocks into your script to construct your story. With a format show, it's likely you'll have a set formula for the script, even specific times or page numbers at which the show moves to its next stage. This puts less pressure on your script, but more pressure on the directing and editing elements.

The example script in Figure 7.1 shows all the different elements you'll need in your script and how to format them.

Your script will go through many different stages:

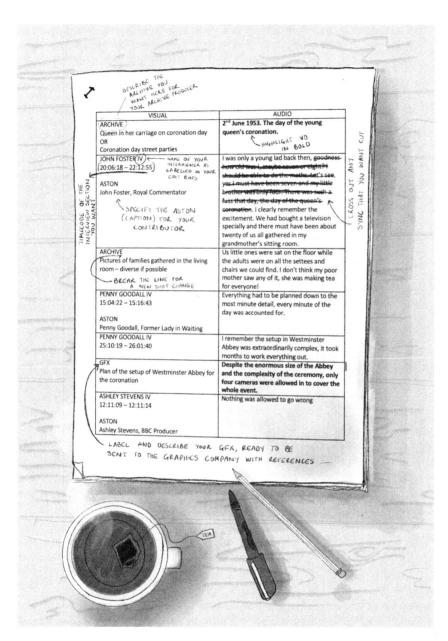

Figure 7.1 Annotated Script.

1. **First draft**. Get the story down. Your first draft is, of course, just the first draft that you submit to the SP – you will need to go through many drafts just to get to the one that's ready to shoot. But this is the stage where you refine your key story points and get the skeleton of what will go in between.

2. **Shooting script**. In this script, you need to add as much detail as possible to help you shoot what you need. Carefully think through what you have your contributors saying and make sure your interview questions are crafted accordingly (see next section). Think through your VISUAL section and make sure you use it to develop a shot list, if needed.

3. **Edit script**. Write this with your edit producer in mind: how do you use your script to communicate to them how you want it to look in the edit?

4. **Timecoded script**. This is the final stage of scripting and you need it to reflect your finished film as closely as possible. Yes, that does mean updating it every time you make a small change to a bit of sync or a visual sequence.

Remember that you're making documentaries. This means that people say things in their own words, not in yours. You can script the VO or comm and the presenter-led pieces, but you can't script the interviews. This is where your interview directing skills will need to come in – you can guide the interviewee to say something that hits your story point in the script, but remember that they will probably say it better than you have written it. Your script is always just a guide – don't be too rigid about it, be open-minded to when something better comes along. This is particularly true of current affairs, obs-docs and reality shows – often something comes up that you haven't bargained for in your script that's considerably better but for which you have to change your structure. It's worth rethinking your structure to accommodate that telly gold.

The best way to learn how to get better at scriptwriting is just to practise. There are scriptwriting courses, guides and tips, but you also need to get some practice in. Start small – maybe a 2-minute film – then build up to a 15-minute film, a half-hour episode, a full hour episode, a 90-minute special. Look at other people's scripts and learn from them, take on board your SP's feedback. This is why in earlier chapters I encouraged you to start writing scripts as early as possible, at AP level. By the time you get to director level, it's too late to learn how to write a script – you already have the responsibility for the finished film resting on your shoulders.

You will need to find yourself a good scriptwriting environment. Some prefer the quiet of working from home, others find a café more inspirational as a location. Often the office is too full of demands or distractions to be

---

What to watch

- Netflix: *Road to Victory*. Have a look at this WW2 series and make a note of the different script elements. Note particularly strong lines of comm. Note exceptional pieces of archive. Observe how the story moves from one subject to the next seamlessly.

---

able to concentrate on writing a proper script. Some people have a particular playlist they like to listen to while scripting. Find your scriptwriting groove and keep it sacred.

Another tip is to watch finished documentaries and imagine them in script form. You could even try transcribing a documentary into a script, formatting it the way it would look as an edit script, with the graphics, archive, comm and interviews all labelled.

Directing interviews

Interviews, whether they're sit-down, two-way between a presenter and contributor, or just asking a contributor questions on the fly, are the backbone of non-scripted television. This section will give you all the advice you need to pull them off well.

Crafting questions

You craft your questions by working backwards from the script. For every story point you need your contributor to hit, you'll create a question that is meant to elicit that answer. You may need a couple of versions of the question in order to get the answer you want – you can either write these multiple versions down or, as you get better at your interview technique, rephrase your questions on the spot as best fits the temperament or style of your contributor. Some people write out their questions one by one for each contributor, but I personally prefer the matrix method: I head into Excel and write down in a spreadsheet all the questions that I'll need to ask my interviewees to cover all the story points in the script.

Then in the columns next to the questions, I put the initials of the interviewees. I'll go down each interviewee column and highlight the box for that question if I think they'll give me a good answer. Different interviewees will have different specialisms – you can't ask everyone everything, otherwise you'll be there for hours, and you'll have too much material at the end. Instead, work out which questions your interviewees will be well suited to and target your questions accordingly. However, do make sure that each question is covered at least twice – that way you'll have multiple options in the edit, and it means if one contributor doesn't answer your question the

Table 7.1 Interview matrix template

QUESTION	AA	BB	CC	DD
NAME, ASTON, DATE, EPISODE NUMBER				
ANSWER IN FULL SENTENCES				
PRESENT TENSE				
ROOM TONE				
QUESTION 1				
QUESTION 2				
QUESTION 3				
QUESTION 4				
QUESTION 5				
QUESTION 6				
QUESTION 7				
QUESTION 8				
QUESTION 9				
QUESTION 10				

way you'd like, you've got another chance to get the material you want with a different contributor. Once you've done all that, your matrix should look something like the one shown in Table 7.1.

As I interview each contributor, I drag their column next to the questions and annotate it as I go through. If they give me a good answer for that question, I'll put a little x in the highlighted box. If they don't give me a good answer, I'll leave it blank. If it's an answer that'll do but I think I can do better with another contributor, I'll write OK. And if they give me an absolute zinger of an answer, I put WOW! (see Table 7.2).

Having all the questions there in the chart adds a certain amount of flexibility to the interview – if you feel they might be suited to another section, you can skip down to that section. Equally, if they're doing really well, you can throw in bonus questions. And having notes from each contributor to hand means you can adjust your other interviews accordingly, making sure that you've got great material for each of your talking points. The chart format means you don't have to write out all your questions every time either, and it's very easy to personalise them for each contributor.

The sit-down interview

This is the easiest kind of interview: you're in a room with two cameras, a microphone on a stand, a DoP and two chairs – one for you and one for

Table 7.2 Example of a completed interview matrix

QUESTION	AA	BB	CC	DD
NAME, ASTON, DATE, EPISODE NUMBER				
ANSWER IN FULL SENTENCES				
PRESENT TENSE				
ROOM TONE				
QUESTION 1	X			
QUESTION 2				
QUESTION 3		OK		
QUESTION 4		X		
QUESTION 5			WOW	
QUESTION 6				
QUESTION 7	X		OK	
QUESTION 8	X			X
QUESTION 9				WOW
QUESTION 10				X

the contributor. When your contributor comes in, make sure they're comfortable and that they have something to drink. You'll need to take some time to adjust the shot for them depending on their height and build; you may also need to touch up their make-up a little (this applies whether they are male or female – no one wants a shiny face in their TV appearance), so make sure you have some translucent powder and a clean brush or make-up sponge to hand.

You should have agreed the shooting style with your SP beforehand, but as a general rule you'll want at least two shots – one straight-on mid-shot, and one close-up side shot. This enables you to cut their interview more easily without having to cut away to anything other than their face. To give you some inspiration on how to frame and set up interview shots, here's a short piece I wrote about the interview styles in three Netflix drama-docs:

Having worked on several drama-docs during my career, I can attest that the balance between the two elements is a tricky one to get right. Netflix has recently made a sterling effort to nail it, with several epic drama-doc series. In this blog, I'm going to look at three of these series on Netflix right now: *Roman Empire*, *Rise of Empires: Ottomans* and *Age of Samurai: Battle for Japan*.

Each one of these has taken a very different approach to the expert interviews, which intercut with the drama and partially narrate it. While most of the budget on these projects tends to be spent on the drama, it's important to get these interviews right as well – it can be jarring if there's a clear difference in production value. Some of these drama-docs tackled the expert interviews better than others...

First up, let's look at *Roman Empire*. This was produced by Stephen David Entertainment (part of Banijay Group, a US-based production conglomerate), and told the story of the Emperor Caligula. Although it could never measure up to the brilliance of the HBO/BBC series *Rome*, its cast of contributors was well put together, drove the story along, and delivered some great takeaway soundbites. The shooting style was very traditional: a warm background with soft focus, plenty of space in the shot for the interviewees to talk into, bright-coloured shirts contrasting against pale faces.

Next, it's *Rise of Empires: Ottomans*. This production by Karga Seven Pictures (LA & Istanbul) delivered a compelling storyline with an engaging cast of characters and fantastic drama sequences with excellent special effects. But the interviews really let the show down. While their cast of contributors was diverse and interesting, it was a very small pool of experts, not all of whom delivered the story in a way that best fit the drama. This necessitated several awkward fast cuts between the three (!) different angles on which the interviews were shot. This was also one too many angles – the back of the head shot in particular caused me several raised eyebrows during what was otherwise a very enjoyable show.

Finally, let's look at *Age of Samurai: Battle for Japan*. Cream Productions in Canada produced this bloody tale of military might that made modern Japan. They opted for a plain black background for their interviews and decided to make them all black-and-white – a style which very effectively complemented the heavily saturated colour palette of the drama, but which only worked because all of their interviewees were either white or Japanese. As well as an over-representation of the pale, male, stale demographic, they cast the contributor net extremely widely indeed, with several different voices narrating each event in the series. As a producer, this struck me as overkill, but when I turned to my partner on the sofa next to me and asked him if he was bothered by it, he said no. A lesson for us producers then – what matters is the content, not the contributors.

Overall, *Age of Samurai: Battle for Japan* had the best interview shooting style, in my opinion. But even that couldn't make up for a weak drama storyline. It looks like Netflix has yet to nail the drama-doc completely!

Once you've approved the shot and the DoP hits record, you'll begin your questions. As you'll have seen at the top of the interview matrix, before you even begin talking about the episode topic, you need to ask them to say:

- Their name (ask them to spell out their surname – and their first name if it's unusual)
- How they would like to be credited
- The date
- Episode number

This will be very useful for the transcripts afterwards – and they serve as easy warm-up questions. As you're asking your episode-related questions, don't be afraid to deviate from your own list – read the room and the contributor, be sensitive to when they don't want to answer a certain question or when they're not giving you the answer you want and just move on to something else. You can always come back to trickier questions at the end. If they're nervous, try to make them feel comfortable – inject a little humour or lightness of touch if you can. Allow them a break after an hour, unless they ask to power through. It is surprisingly exhausting answering questions in front of a camera! Try to be encouraging too, unless this is a very serious current affairs interview! If they're doing well, nod or smile or say 'that was great'. It really helps build a strong, positive relationship with your contributor – which will be very useful for you if they're good and you want to work with them again.

The two-way interview

This style of interview is conducted between a presenter and a contributor. You'll need a two-camera setup, one on the contributor and one on the presenter – but the most important shot is the contributor. Save your best camera for the new face and use your second camera just to get the reactions and questions from the presenter. The most popular style of two-way interview uses an over-the-shoulder style to capture a bit of the presenter together with the contributor, and the same in reverse, but recently more and more directors have been playing with this style, even incorporating some of the lighting, microphone and general setup into the frame. If you're just starting out in your directing career, stick to the classic method, but watch carefully for how other directors have done it and develop your own style over time.

While the visual setup can be fairly straightforward, you will need to double down on the audio. Both your presenter and contributor will need lapel mics, plus a boom mic in between them. It's much more logistically difficult to redo a two-way interview than a single sit-down one, so you need to try and get as much right first time as possible!

What to watch

Look out for different two-way interview styles in the following documentaries:

- Channel 5: *Eight Days that Made Rome* with Bettany Hughes
- BBC Four: *Sound of TV* with Neil Brand
- BBC Two: *The Princes and the Press* with Amol Rajan

In terms of conducting the interview, the pressure is off you – the presenter will lead the questions. Depending on the calibre of the presenter, they may need to have their questions scripted in advance or they will be experienced and professional enough to ask their own questions in their own style. The latter is infinitely preferable, but make sure you have a chat with the presenter as early in the production process as possible to establish your working method. You should keep notes during the interview though, just to double-check that all the story points have been hit, and flag it gently with the presenter at the end of the interview in case you need to cover a few more points.

In addition to the interview setup, you will also need some introductory shots of the presenter with the contributor: for example, the contributor could be playing the piano, or walking through a garden with the presenter, or showing the presenter a painting – whatever is relevant to the subsequent topic of the interview. These are used under the VO section that will introduce the interview – and can also be helpful for cutting in between parts of the interview. When you're establishing your location for the two-way interview, keep in mind that it will need to be suitable for these actuality shots, too.

On the fly

Whether you're getting vox pops for a news story or grabbing some sync as you walk with a contributor on an obs-doc, your priorities for getting the interviews change when your filming environment is less controlled. The most important thing at this stage is to get good sound and to get as much of their face in the shot as possible. The viewer is surprisingly forgiving of camera wobbles and dodgy focus – as long as the content and story is compelling and it fits the overall aesthetic of the production.

Let's hear from Sophie Smith on her tips for shooting on the fly:

If you're shooting interviews on the fly, you have to be sensitive to your surroundings and the people you're working with. If you can, build a strong rapport with people in advance of filming as this really helps on the day. Explain what you need from them and why you need it – people are much more amenable when they understand what you're trying to achieve. This is especially important when you have to film the same thing more than once. Stop for short breaks if they appear tired or restless. Timing can be hard to keep tabs on in the moment – I often delegate timings to my AP to make sure I stick as closely as possible to the schedule and cover everything I need. Always think of the edit when you're filming and make sure you're covered for shots. You don't always need to be too literal but GVs and cutaways related to the interview are essential in most cases and go a long way in the edit.

Directing actuality: interview with Marta Garcia Aliaga

Ask yourself the question – what is it that you're trying to achieve in this shoot? I find it helpful to create a daily shot and sync list in accordance with my shooting script (or paper edit, if you're shooting actuality after you've recorded your interviews). Ask yourself what you need to get out of each day, and make a simple list that you can go back to, tick off and consult whenever you're unsure of what to do next.

You might want to classify this list into (at least) three categories:

1. Shots and sync you need
2. Shots and sync you would like
3. Bonus shots and sync

You are responsible for making sure that (1) is in the can before you return to base, but it's always great if you can also come home with (2) and (3).

Doing a daily pre-shoot briefing with everyone involved is key. This includes any crew, presenters or reporters and contributors. If you are working with a reporter or presenter, brief them beforehand about any topics you need to cover. Most experienced reporters/presenters won't need it, but many do find it helpful to have these written down. Daily briefings are also a good opportunity to mic up your contributors, reporters or presenters. Do check that your sound is clear, not rattly, and that your levels aren't (and this is, of course, a technical term) all over the place.

If you are able to nudge your contributors, try to do so before you start filming. For example, if you're filming them at a protest, ask them what they expect might happen, and to what degree they are going to get involved. (This should have already been discussed prior to the shoot if you knew about this event, particularly from a safety perspective, but if you're working with a story that's unfolding quickly, it might have just cropped up!). Brief them about what would help you to cover that protest properly, and what you need from them – but remember to always be respectful and avoid interfering with their business, or putting them in harm's way, of course. You're there to tell their story at the end of the day.

If you are flying solo, you'll have to make sure you're listening while you film, and, when appropriate, you will need to nudge your contributors with any thoughts or questions you think are not covered yet. I know, I know, it's tricky! But a skill we all develop with time and experience.

Remember you're filming sequences, not just standalone shots, so you will need plenty of establishing shots. These could be filmed outside the building you're filming in, and go along with some GVs of the street it's on (ideally with, for example, moving people, flapping flags, cars etc). It's often helpful to have drone shots to go with them too. Filmed conversations also need to have a visual beginning and end. If you've missed the start, you might need to come up with a creative way to make up for it. A 'way in' can be something as simple as the reporter or presenter walking or driving towards a meeting and telling us who they're about to do something with and why. If you don't have a reporter/presenter, you could get the contributor walking into the building, up some stairs to the place where you will be filming with them.

Now we're into the actuality. Make sure to watch around you – shooting actuality is similar to people-watching. Ask yourself again, what is it that you are after? How can you best capture your story? Are you filming dialogue – two people having a difficult conversation, for example? Make sure you're not just focusing on whoever is speaking at the time, but also catching the facial expressions of the other. Filming hand movements is helpful, but don't overdo it – faces are generally much more important as they won't be repeated. If you're shooting the conversation with just one camera, don't ping pong between people, try to find natural points of inflexion to switch between them.

Stick to your trusty zoom lens to best follow the action and get as close to your subjects as possible – about 1-2 metres away. As a priority, focus on what's happening in front of you – remember you can crack out your set of prime lenses to pick up objects and establishers later, after the actuality has finished. When you're doing these pickups, you can always ask people to stand in again, if that's an option.

Final tips:
- Once you think you have enough GVs, shoot between five and ten more
- Make sure your sound is working! Always test it before you shoot!
- Pick up atmospheric sound and room tone

But, most importantly:

- Don't panic! Keeping as calm as you can will help. After all – it's only telly
- Remember to have fun in the process!

Directing drama: interview with Jeremy Turner

Drama reconstructions come in a variety of forms, from abstract images that are more evocative than illustrative to full-on scripted drama with lavish locations, complex art direction and big casts of actors. Regardless of its scale, the fundamentals of directing drama are the same.

Script

Most of my directing is done at the writing stage. By focusing your creative efforts into the script, directing on location should be a case of painting by numbers, leaving you time to work with the actors and the various departments of the film crew.

Drama scripts tend to have a set format, designed to help the flow of the storytelling as well as inform all the key logistical and technical consider-ations that will need to be passed on to the different people tasked with organising cast, booking locations, building sets, cameras, lighting, etc.

This is an example of a drama script written for the series *Web of Lies*:

EXT. ANDY FINCH'S HOUSE – STREET – NIGHT
Across the street from Andy Finch's house, A POLICE OFFICER (division TBA), armed with a RIFLE (make TBA), watches ANDY step onto the porch tentatively raising his hands above his head.

BRENDAN JONES (INTERVIEW VO)
Swattings create incredibly dangerous situations, everyone is on edge while carrying instruments of death in their hands.
There is a moment of calm outside Andrew Finch's house. Then, Andrew lowers one hand, perhaps to pull up his pants.

BANG.
The sound of a single rifle shot shatters the night air.
In slo-mo Andrew Finch crashes to the floor.

From this part of the script we know most of the important details to set up the shoot on the day:

- The location
- Time of day
- The action
- The main characters
- Key props
- How the scene ties back to the testimony of the interviewee

NB: Other elements (descriptions of Andy: his clothes, the type of house and neighbourhood he lives in and the other cops surrounding the house were set up earlier in the script).

One note on scripting is always try and get in and out of a scene as quickly and as effectively as possible. Does a scene, shot in a restaurant, really need a whole set up with a car arriving, people getting out of the car, walking in, etc.? Or could following a waiter carrying a plate from the kitchen to the table do the job just as well?

Different departments

Having written the script, the next stage is to break it down into the component parts. Ideally, this is done by the first assistant director (aka the first AD, or just 'the first'), and the relevant information passed on to the different heads of department (HoDs). To list (and explain) all the various roles in a film crew would be long and tedious (the length of the end credits on a movie will give you some idea of just how many people can be involved), but roughly speaking a drama film crew falls into these departments:

- The camera department, headed up by the DoP (or cinematographer)
- Electric and lighting – the HoD here is the 'gaffer'
- Grip (camera mounting and rigging equipment) – HoD is the key grip
- Sound – HoD is the production sound mixer
- Art department – HoD is the production designer and/or art director
- Locations – locations manager
- Hair and make-up – key make-up designer
- Costume – costume designer
- Casting – casting director

If any special effects (such as pyrotechnics), visual effects (like CGI elements or green screen filming), aerial/drone filming or stunts are needed, then further specialists can be brought in.

As the drama director you will, at some stage, end up talking to all of these HoDs, usually in a pre-production meeting, but the main line of communication to all these people will be through the first AD, who will then liaise with their ADs (second, third and so on, depending on the scale of the production). It is also the role of the ADs to make sure you don't fall behind schedule on a filming day and to organise the principal (and background) cast through costume, hair and make-up. Your first AD will (hopefully) become your best friend, for the duration of the shoot at least.

Breaking the script down

Once the script has been signed off, the first AD will be able to break it down to its component form and pass the information to each of the HoDs so they can start organising what's needed for filming to take place. Dedicated scriptwriting software, such as Final Draft, can make the job quicker and easier as it's designed to be compatible with production organising systems like Movie Magic.

After the HoDs have had a bit of time to think about what's needed and to start coming up with suggestions, you can start to have pre-production meetings. These meetings allow the director to explain their vision of the cast, the look and feel of the visuals – both from a filming standpoint and the art direction – as well as discuss any key technical aspects such as specialist props, vehicles or green screen filming.

To help with this the script can be supplemented with storyboards, mood boards and visual references from other productions you like the look of.

With so many factors in play, having a detailed script and being very organised will make your life a lot easier in the long run.

Casting

In drama scenes where you are featuring actors, you'll go through the process of casting. This usually requires writing a short scene for the actors to perform during the audition. Ideally, you'll sit with the casting director, another person who will operate the camera to capture the performance, and someone else to sign the actors in, give them the scripts and make sure they fill in their information correctly. Be warned, casting actors can be a strange business: you'll come across headshots that look nothing like the person standing in front of you, performances that take eccentricity to a whole new level – and always be wary of actors who come in wearing costumes. On the other hand, castings can be a joy to behold: actors, young and old, who bring the script to life and breathe genuine emotion and resonance into words that you wrote sitting on your sofa weeks earlier.

Location and tech recces

If you're filming on location (as opposed to a studio shoot), you will need to take to the road to find your ideal settings; these 'recces' (or 'scouts', as the Americans call them) will be organised by the locations manager. It's also good to have (assuming they are not snowed under by scheduling everything) the first AD (or if not them, one of the ADs) and the DoP by your side. Recces can be long days, stuck in a car, but I love looking for locations, mainly because I'm super nosy, but also because it's the first time I get to see my ideas become some sort of reality.

When you've found your locations, you will then revisit them, with as many HoDs as possible, on a 'tech recce'. From the perspective of the creative departments, this is their chance to ask you about how they can make the setting match your vision as closely as possible. For the more technical departments it's their opportunity to work out where the power will come from, what grip equipment will work best and even if extra toilet facilities are required. As the director your main focus is the on the creative side, but it's also worth keeping an ear out for things like parking, as it could ruin your dream of a drone shot or maintaining the idea that the scene is being shot at the turn of the 19th century.

Filming days

By the time filming finally comes around, there's a good chance you will be fatigued by all the thousands of questions you've had to answer, late-night sessions rewriting the script because there's not enough time or money to shoot the original one, and last-minute casting sessions, because finding someone to play a 15th-century French warrior-turned-Satanist hasn't proved as straightforward as you'd have hoped.

But all the tiredness usually washes away when you turn up and see the cameras and lights being set up, the art department transforming the location into, say, an '80s gangster hideout or medieval torture chamber, the actors going through their lines and an AD taking your breakfast order.

There can be a temptation to start getting people to hurry up, because setting up drama shoots can be a slow process – there are a lot of people and a lot of moving parts; but that is not your job – pushing the day through is the first AD's thing. Use the time to say 'Hi' to the HoDs, to get to know people's names and sit with the actors to build up a rapport with them. A moment will come when the first AD will ask you to 'block out' the first scene. Blocking is when you get the actors to play out the scene in the place where you want to film it. It can be a bit unnerving because, as well as working out where and how the actors should walk, talk and interact with each other and the world they now occupy, it's also a chance for the HoDs (and the rest of their teams) to plan the best place to put cameras, choose lenses, position lights, build the grip equipment, hide sound gear, set props and the rest, so all eyes are on you. This is why having the first AD and the DoP accompany you on the location recces can be so useful, because you can have a sneaky practice when there is nobody else there to see you. Having worked through the scene with the cast and the crew, you can start planning the next scene with the first AD, or running lines with the actors who have been through the 'works' (hair, make-up and costume), or have five minutes to yourself and finish off the now cold coffee that you started over an hour ago.

With everything set, you can go for the first take. The director should have their own monitor, although, budget depending, you may have to share it with at least one HoD, most likely the DoP. The first AD now runs the show – they will make sure everyone is set, final checks have been done and call 'action'. The first take is usually little more than a full rehearsal, but I like to make sure the rehearsal is filmed – you never know, you might get it first take. The odds are you won't. But you never know. If you are filming scripted drama, your main job as the director is to feed back to the actors, to get the best performance and to make sure they are happy with everything. The next priority is to work with crew to discuss camera moves and lighting, as well as any changes needed in the hair and make-up (H&MU), costume and art departments.

Once the first scene is completed, you just keep moving on to the next scene, then the next...

Workflow

By having a good script, you should know what you need from a drama scene; this means you should avoid the temptation to run an entire scene over and over again, trying to get the perfect one-shot take. I like to start with the wide 'master' shot, and run as much of the action in a single take as possible, but if there is a fluff, rather than starting from the beginning I will get the actors to pick up the action, until we have got to the end of the action. If you have a script supervisor, they will be able to tell you which bits you need to cover with the close-ups to ensure the scene will edit seamlessly. If you don't have a 'scripty', then try and get a member of the production team to help; otherwise you'll need to mark up your own script.

Don't panic

Every director has their own way of doing things, but, no matter how stressful things get, I strongly believe there is no place for shouting or finger pointing on set. If there are problems, identify ways of solving them calmly. There have been (rare) occasions where I've had actors completely forget their lines and start to panic as a result, or when key bits of camera gear have failed, and neither situation would've been helped by raised voices. By taking the actor into a quiet room and going through their lines with them, they regained their confidence and delivered a standout performance for the rest of the day. With the broken camera situation, we spent the time waiting for the replacement part by blocking through the following scenes, so only a little time was lost. If the day does start to get away from you, it's always a good idea to identify the scenes you can film as simply as possible (in my case, this is going into 'documentary mode', stick a zoom lens on and go handheld). And, as a last resort, always have a Plan D – i.e. know which scenes you can drop that will have the least impact on the overall story.

Directing presenters

Much of this is about developing a personal dynamic with the presenter. If you work well together, the production process – which can be stressful and exhausting – will run much more smoothly. However, it takes time and experience to build up a strong relationship with a presenter; mostly you will be working with a new presenter every time, flung into these situations with barely an introduction. This section will cover both tips for building that personal dynamic, as well as the key shots you will need to get with your presenter and how to direct them in each of those scenarios.

Building a personal relationship

In general, there are two types of presenter you'll be working with (experienced or fresh) and they will serve one of two purposes in the programme. Either the programme or series is fully presenter-led, or the presenter simply serves as a voice through which to convey information.

You will develop a stronger relationship with the presenter if they are fully leading the series. The presenters on these kinds of series are usually experienced, which means they will be professional in terms of their delivery on camera and it will take less time to get the shots you need with them, but may be a large personality off screen, which you will need to manage carefully. Make sure you carve out some time before you start shooting together to meet them for coffee, discuss their views on the series and the scripts, and find out any preferences they have during filming, particularly in terms of how they like to receive direction, and most importantly – dietary requirements (make sure you pass this information on to production management and your AP). Having this chat BEFORE you shoot will save a lot of time in those first few days as you're working out your dynamic – plus, the presenter will appreciate the effort you've taken to get to know them and consider their working style. It's also a good idea to reach out to any colleagues who have worked with that presenter before and get their tips.

You will spend less time with a facilitator-presenter, but they may be less experienced in front of the camera so will need a little more direction and encouragement, at least at the start of your journey together. The types of programmes that use these presenters are usually fairly fast-turnaround, so you may not have time to sit down for a proper get-to-know-you session – that said, you should at the very least have a phone call with the presenter

What to watch

For examples of programmes or series which are fully presenter-led, look at:

- BBC Four: *Write Around the World* with Richard E. Grant
- Smithsonian: *Mystic Britain* with Mary-Ann Ochota and Clive Anderson
- ITV: Joanna Lumley's *Silk Road Adventure*
- Channel 4: *From Russia to Iran* with Levison Wood
- BBC Two: *Turkey* with Simon Reeve
- BBC One: *Who Do You Think You Are?*

For examples of programmes or series through which the presenter conveys information, look at:

- *Countryfile* (BBC One)
- *What on Earth?* (Discovery Channel)

in advance. They may also be more inclined to come and meet you at the office, which would save you a bit of time. In this situation, rather than getting their views on the scripts and series, you should be briefing them on the format, the shooting schedule and what you expect from them. Ask them about their experience, how they've found filming on previous series (from which you might be able to glean a bit about their working style) and their dietary requirements (again, pass this information on to production management and your AP).

Why the emphasis on dietary requirements? Well, as I hope I've made clear in previous chapters, food is the most important thing on a shoot. Keeping your crew hydrated and fed is paramount to a smooth, professional shoot. If your presenter is a strict vegetarian and you are shooting in a country that thinks chicken counts as a vegetarian option, you will need to take extra care when planning where your crew is staying and eating. If they don't eat pork and you are shooting in East Asia, you will need to brief your fixer carefully to check that there is no pork in the food. If they have fatal allergies and you cannot always double-check what's in the food they're being served, you will need to know what to do in case of an allergic reaction and have planned accordingly. If you are filming in very remote locations where their dietary requirements cannot be catered for, you will need to help them plan in advance and bring some of their own sustenance. You cannot let your presenter go hungry – not on your watch. You need to care about them and for them because you need them to perform well for you. Especially when the series is entirely presenter-led, they are indispensable. If you show that you care about them, they will feel well disposed towards you and you will have a stronger working relationship – which means better telly as a result.

Filming presenters

There are eight key types of sequences you'll need to capture if you're making a presenter-led documentary:

1. **The Two-Way Interview.** This is where the presenter introduces and then interviews someone, such as an expert or witness. See the section on Interviews for more details.

2. **The Talking Head Interview.** This is just a mid-shot of an expert making a relevant point, with a caption appearing at the bottom of the screen.

3. **Two-Way Exploration.** The presenter is taken around a site, or shown an object of interest, while a resident expert explains the significance of that object or place.

4. **Walking PTC Exploring a Site.** This is where the presenter explores a site or shows an object and explains it by themselves.

5. **Walking PTC Storytelling.** The presenter walks through a neutral or themed location (e.g. along a path, in front of some ancient-looking columns, down a corridor flanked by paintings etc.) while they tell a part of the story of the documentary.

6. **Static PTC.** The presenter is sitting down, or standing still, relating another part of the story, or making an important point.

7. **Presenter on a Journey.** This is quite self-explanatory – short sequences of the presenter in a car, on a boat, in a helicopter, cycling – whatever you like – to show them on their way from one location to another. This is particularly important if your documentary takes you to locations all around the world – although it's perfectly possible to snap from the presenter in front of the Parthenon to a sewer in Tunisia, sometimes it can feel like a sudden and disjointed transition. Journey shots help to smooth it out, and allow for some explanatory narration over the scenic shot.

8. **Wallpaper Shots.** These are non-sync (not talking) shots of the presenter walking along, or big sweeping landscape shots, or aerial drone footage, or close-ups (cutaways) of objects, flowers, road signs – whatever you need to fill in some narration time, or just some contemplating

time in your documentary. Remember, you can never have too many of these!

Golden Rule: don't skimp on the cutaways or GVs! Always allow a bit of extra time to capture more of these at your filming location. If you have a super-keen AP who wants to get more shooting experience, ask them to capture some more GVs – whether that's on a proper second camera, on a cute portable A7S or even on a GoPro – whatever your budget allows.

What to watch

Watch all the presenter-led documentaries cited as examples in this section and note down these eight sequences when you spot them. Study the creative ways that each director has chosen to film these sequences and evaluate which work better.

Appendix

This appendix is a collection of anecdotes from our contributors, describing difficult situations they've encountered during their time in television – whether that's the challenges of freelancing, solving unforeseen difficulties on a shoot, discrimination in the workplace or unpleasant team dynamics. The purpose of this appendix is threefold: to prepare new entrants for potentially difficult situations they may encounter, to highlight endemic issues within the TV industry and to show that it's not all sunshine and roses (or red carpets and wrap parties). It's designed to prepare, rather than put off – every industry has its difficulties and unpleasant characters; TV is no different. However, what we can change is how we deal with those difficult situations. Always report bullying and harassment at work – it is always unacceptable.

DEALING WITH AGGRESSIVE COLLEAGUES

Will Taylor-Gammon, runner

An assistant producer needed to sit at a particular computer so they could access documents on that specific desktop. However, an executive producer was sitting there, working on their laptop, while listening to music. I tapped them on the shoulder and politely asked if they could briefly move. However, before I could finish explaining why someone needed access to the PC they were sitting at, they aggressively told me to go away as they were trying to work. They put their headphones back on and went back to working. I then tapped them on the shoulder again, and this time they stood up and shouted at me to leave them alone so they could work.

Unfortunately, in a lot of industries you might work with rude people who are unnecessarily aggressive. At this moment I stayed calm and told my manager what had happened. My manager then spoke to the managing director about the situation. The executive producer who shouted at me was spoken to, and asked my manager to send me

DOI: 10.4324/9781003294009-9

their apologies. I was frustrated that the executive producer did not come to me to apologise in person, but I recognised that this was a step in the right direction.

LEARNING TO SAY NO

Emily Mayson, archive producer

We fight so hard to get into and move up in this industry; it becomes part of our identity. As freelancers, we feel like we are constantly auditioning for our next job. There's always too much work to do and we pressure ourselves to do it all and do it well. Because of all this, we have a tendency to become workaholics. In response to the fear that we may never work again, we prioritise work above all else and become social commitment phobes – missing holidays, weddings, birthdays… even doctor's appointments. It's difficult to have a work–life balance. The job is all-encompassing.

I've learned the hard way that sometimes you have to say no. At one company, I was working on seven projects at once. It was relentless for months. I worked all hours and still didn't feel like I was doing any project justice. One week I was paid for a nine-day week – six days and three all-nighters. It destroyed my mental and physical health. I often worked from home because I hated going to the office – not only did my commute waste valuable work time and my colleagues provide unwanted distractions, but I was so unhappy, I feared I might throw myself under a train on the way there. I ended up quitting. They replaced me with three people. With budgets being squeezed, production companies must cut corners where they can. I've learned not to let my wellbeing become the hidden cost of that.

SHOOTING OUTSIDE THE BOX

Alec Lindsell, shooting PD

Everyone had a difficult time during the pandemic. Continuing television production when not being able to be in the same place as the people you were filming was probably the greatest difficulty in the industry. When Covid hit, I was working on *Inside the Tower of London* for Lion TV: a behind-the-scenes show detailing the inner workings of one of the capital's most popular tourist attractions, with some added historical content thrown in.

As we started filming, visitor numbers at the Tower dwindled until, like all tourist attractions around the country, it was forced to close its doors. We still wanted to capture the goings-on at the Tower even though the doors were closed to the public and thankfully, as most productions did, we were able to rely on UGC (user-generated content) from the Beefeaters (the Tower guards). But these men and women were ex-military and not used to filming content for television. On our first attempts, the footage coming back was…well, as expected from non-professionals, but we felt it was important to document the fact that the ancient ceremonies at the Tower were still being carried out behind closed doors, despite the pandemic.

As I was not able to be there in person due to lockdown, and some of my early efforts to explain what we needed via the press office had not really worked, I decided to try and solve the problem by making the Beefeaters a series of "how to" videos on my own mobile phone. I wanted to give them enough of the basics so that it was easy for them to follow but also would provide us with good footage to use in the show. I broke the videos down into things like:

- Framing
- The best way to hold the camera
- How best to talk directly into the camera for a video diary
- How to shoot cutaways of the areas or things they were talking about

And included some other tips, such as:

- Holding for a five-count before stopping recording

I then went to some nearby woodlands with my phone and filmed myself doing all these things, edited the videos down, wrote up a sheet on how best to transfer the footage to the edit without losing quality, and sent this off. The results were great! The Beefeaters really took to it and the footage we got back (barring one or two cutaways that had been filmed in portrait and not landscape) was excellent. We were then able to create an entire section of an episode which really was behind locked doors at the Tower of London. This was an example of directing from afar by giving enough clear information that our contributors could take it in and execute it well, without overloading them with requests and confusing them with jargon or technical requirements.

KNOWING YOUR WORTH

Emily Mayson, archive producer

We need to talk about money. I (female) discovered that my (male) holiday cover got paid £100 a day more than me, and he only worked on one of my three projects. A kind production manager warned me I was being underpaid. When I talked to my colleagues about it, I found the men had the attitude of 'ask for a £100 rise on a new job, expect to get £50'. The women asked for a £25 raise and hoped they'd say yes, but would accept a no, thinking they were being cheeky. It's important to ask your peers and production manager friends for advice and look at union guidelines. Work out what the going rate is for your role and experience. You don't want to price yourself out of a job. Equally, you don't want to undercut your peers and set a precedent of low rates. Don't devalue your role. Make sure you are getting a fair rate for your work. If several people are doing the same role on a project, compare notes and demand equal pay.

USING YOUR NETWORK

Jules Walker, production manager

I arrived on a production as line producer/production manager mid-production. There was a team in the US shooting various content/interviews. It was a tight schedule across three weeks. Within the first week the camera assistant/2nd camera unit needed to return to the UK. With a shoot schedule in place, production needed to source a 2nd camera unit/camera assistant with very short lead times and little time to vet crew. On top of this, the shoot was during the pandemic so there was an additional layer of Health & Safety to consider. This is where the production black book of contacts becomes very useful! Crew are generally a very helpful group of folks and through networking and Facebook groups we managed to source crew for each shoot day. It was a constant KBS [kick, b*****k, scramble] but we managed it, making further contacts for the black book of contacts too.

Conclusion

I hope this book has given you a strong grounding in what the editorial ladder of Factual TV looks like and how to climb it. Remember that your career may not be linear – and that's OK. The most important consideration is to work on projects that you enjoy. If that's not possible for whatever reason (and the fact of the matter is that there will be some projects you don't enjoy), make sure that you learn something from every project you work on. That has been my philosophy, and tracking what I have learned from each of my projects has led to this book.

The television industry is not perfect. This book is trying to fix one of those imperfections: by making it easier to break into and more accessible for a wider audience. TV still needs to fix its burnout issues, its lack of a supportive career structure, its dearth of mentoring opportunities, its diversity problem. I hope that through the appendix, I have prepared you for some of these issues and encouraged you to do your bit to help fix them when you come across them. Together, I hope we can make TV a less exploitative, more open and more rewarding industry.

Through TV, you have the potential to meet interesting, sometimes powerful people. You could travel the world. You could pioneer a new filming style or break cutting-edge stories. You could influence policy, behaviour, society. Your story can change minds and mindsets. You can teach people new things and raise awareness of important issues. You can entertain people too: you can be their comfort at the end of a long day, their refuge from the pressures of the world.

You will look at the world in a new way. You will develop storytelling and project management skills that will set you up for many other lucrative and rewarding careers, should you decide to leave TV. You will develop a unique understanding of media, influence and communication – which, in our current world, is the cornerstone of not only daily interactions but even geopolitics.

DOI: 10.4324/9781003294009-10

Index

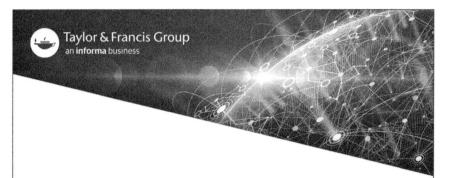

Printed in Great Britain
by Amazon

26502003R00097